OUTNUMBERED

D1501352

DIANE GRONKOWSKI

PAGE PUBLISHING
Conneaut Lake, PA

First originally published by Page Publishing 2022

ISBN 978-1-6624-5590-2 (pbk)
ISBN 978-1-6624-5591-9 (digital)

Printed in the United States of America

WELCOME TO THE JUNGLE

Before I became a parent, my résumé was a simple one pager. One year into marriage, I added "mother" to my work experience and had no idea I was about to embark on the most intensive on-the-job training of my life. I wouldn't dream that raising five boisterous little humans, all to become professional athletes, would help me acquire the patience of a saint and a skill set to rival that of any corporate executive. Oh, but it did. By the time my kids were grown and had flown, I had developed the ability to manage seven independent lives, cook for an army, do my own plumbing and car repair, diagnose childhood illnesses, recite a dozen teams' statistics, and develop a useful system for keeping socks in pairs in the laundry. In a little over three decades, I learned a lot about manipulating and encouraging often-obstinate young people, budgeting on a budget, toddler psychology, stinky team logistics, culinary arts for the masses, sports medicine for those who won't admit they are hurting, and motivational speaking for adults and children. The things I know that my children learned well are problem-solving, creativity, and perseverance.

I have five boys, each born two years apart. I went from changing diapers to toilet training to changing diapers to toilet training to buying jockey shorts then athletic supporters, to now, where I'm changing diapers for grandchildren. I went from practice to practice to game to practice to game to game to game. I did laundry daily—heck, hourly—and cleaned the house as I went. I shopped for groceries and cooked breakfast, lunch, snacks, and dinner. Press repeat many, many times, as my boys went from weighing a collective total of 39 pounds at birth growing into tall, big, strong guys, now weighing all together over half a ton, each having become a professional athlete! And I did all the many jobs of parenthood without thinking much about them. Don't get me wrong, I wouldn't change a thing. I see now how my time as a mom with kids at home was so precious and short. And I know that, for much of that time, really *all* of it, I was very, very tired.

Since the joyful delivery of son number one, I have added expertise and titles to my résumé, including project manager, chauffeur, social coordinator, nurse, conflict negotiator, bookkeeper, officer in charge of waste management, event planner, director of physical plant, travel agent, and early childhood development specialist. While I knew how to make sure they all brushed their teeth and flossed regularly, cooking for a crowd, understanding the finer points of ice hockey, and managing five conflicting schedules were not things I expected to know how to do. When a new situation came up—weekly, daily, hourly—I think the most important skill I developed is adaptability. By the time son number five came on the scene, I had become a master of organization and was not easily fazed by the permanent commotion at the Gronkowski house and was keenly aware of my position as the only female team member. I am indeed outnumbered.

Did I have any idea that I was raising five future professional athletes? Of course not. Sometimes, as they grew and challenged one another and beat on one another in that brotherly way so typical of my rowdy crew, I would pause and wonder what they would become. Among the strewn sofa cushions, muddy sneakers, basketballs, and scattered matchbox cars, could there be a future president of the United States?

I'm writing this book to set the record straight: the success of my boys is simply the result of hard work, dedication, love, and true teamwork.

I consider myself fortunate to have been able to stay home with my children as they grew up. I didn't miss working outside the home, but I surely learned that it's possible to be lonely while never being alone. I came to realize that while this work is important and incredibly exhausting, it comes with so many unmeasurable rewards. There is no paycheck or pension. Nor are there awards for changing the most diapers in a ten-year span or for consistently getting everyone everywhere they need to be, on time and dressed in the right gear. In the end, I have earned a mighty-mom trophy indeed: all five of my boys achieved their goals of becoming professional athletes—four to the NFL and one in the MLB. As adults, now only one remaining in the NFL, they continue to achieve their goals in business, as fathers and partners, and as excellent role models for the young people who watch them so closely. I could not be prouder of them all.

In this book, I get to tell my story of raising five rambunctious boys to be successful, thriving men, all of whom worked their way to the top in athletics, signing professional sports contracts, and carrying on afterward with successful careers. I give football fans a glimpse into the childhood of their favorite New England Patriots, now Tampa Bay Buccaneers, tight end, Rob Gronkowski. But more than anything, my story offers parents inspiration, helpful takeaways, and tips about keeping their cherubs fed and outfitted, managing their schedules, their schoolwork and growing needs while making sure they are at activities, practice and games on time, dealing with the heartbreak of losing, sibling squabbles, and maintaining sanity amid the chaos, that I wished someone might have shared with me when I was home alone with my boys!

Outnumbered, an inside look at my fraternity, is important to me because I feel that the humble role of parent to the high achievers and the publicly adored is often overlooked. I know I played an important part in each of my children's lives, and I know there are many parents out there who don't even realize the tremendous impact they have on their own offspring. This is my side of the story, and I'm happy to be able to tell it, for myself and for all the parents who don't get the credit they deserve.

I always smile when I see someone on TV, a professional athlete or even a kid in a commercial, wave at the camera and say, "Hi, Mom!" Most of the time, you can't actually hear the words, but it is easy to read their lips. I know how I felt, and still feel, when one of my sons gives me that smile, wave, thumbs-up acknowledgment of *me*. When I notice others grinning for the camera and mouthing "Hi, Mom," I wonder who she is. That lucky mother! I feel joy for her, and I think, *Good for you!* Good for you for your child's success, and good for you that your child recognizes your importance.

In raising these five amazing boys, I have been accused of having a secret superpower. This may be true. I do think it takes superpower efforts to raise kids. All parents have the ability to do what I did. Really. Today, all my sons are successful, independent adults. Some of them welcome me to continue in my support role. Some of them do not, and that's okay with me. My joy as their mother is getting to witness them heading off in their own directions and moving forward, step-by-step in their lives. I believe this is the greatest reward for any parent. I'm truly blessed.

It wasn't until my youngest was off to college and out of the house that I really took stock of what it means to be a parent: the many, many tasks undertaken, the skills learned and mastered to get those babies to adulthood. It's the hardest job in the world, the most rewarding, and I'm thrilled to lay it out play-by-play (pun intended) for parents everywhere.

5 boys sitting under kitchen counter

GRONKOWSKI TEAM ROSTER

Diane Gronkowski Walters – stay-at-home mom, team captain, nutrition manager, academic coach, chauffeur, wardrobe specialist, travel planner, spiritual leader, health care guru, grandmother
Born: September 24, 1960, Buffalo, NY
Height: 5'6"
School: Erie Community College, dental technology
Professional sports: 18 years and counting, NFL mom; six years, MLB.
Today: Lives in Florida with husband, Mike Walters, where they run
   a very successful Home Watch business.

Gordie Gronkowski Jr.—much-revered oldest brother, "the mayor"
Born: June 26, 1983, Buffalo, NY
Height: 6'5"
Weight: 248 lbs.
Birth weight: 7 lbs.
School: Jacksonville University, degree in business. Freshman All-
   American baseball.
Professional sports: Drafted by Major League Baseball Los Angeles
   Angels 2006; moved to minor leagues where he played for 6
   years before retiring with an injury.
Today: Lives in Boston, MA, and works in sales for family business,
   Gronk Fitness. Is launching a vitamin drink called Vue.

Dan Gronkowski—the organizer, first to play football
Born: January 21, 1985, Amherst, NY
Height: 6'5"
Weight: 265 lbs.
Birth weight: 7 lbs., 6 oz.
School: University of Maryland, degree in marketing. Earned an MBA and nominated as a Rhodes Scholar.
Professional sports: Drafted by NFL Detroit Lions 2009; Denver Broncos 2010; joined New England Patriots in 2011 and played two games with younger brother Rob before joining the Cleveland Browns for 2011 and 2012 seasons.
Today: Married, four children. Lives in Buffalo, NY, and works for family business.

Chris Gronkowski—quiet, brotherly battle instigator, entrepreneur
Born: December 26, 1986, Buffalo, NY
Height: 6'2"
Weight: 250 lbs.
Birth weight: 7 lbs., 14 oz.
School: Recruited by the University of Maryland, played two football seasons, then transferred to the University of Arizona to play football and earn an accounting degree.
Professional sports: Signed with NFL Dallas Cowboys in 2010. Picked up by Indianapolis Colts in 2011 then traded to Denver Broncos in 2012. In 2013 signed with San Diego Chargers before retiring because of injury.
Today: Married, four children. Lives in Dallas where he launched Ice Shaker in 2017. He and his brothers successfully pitched the business to Alex Rodriguez and Mark Cuban on the Shark Tank TV show. Chris and his wife, Brittany, also have an online business, EverythingDecorated.com.

Rob Gronkowski—"Gronk," comic relief, always smiling
Born: May 14, 1989, Amherst, NY
Height: 6'6"
Weight: 269 lbs.
Birth weight: 8 lbs., 14 oz.
School: University of Arizona where he played football with brother
Chris. Degree incomplete as he was drafted by the NFL New
England Patriots in 2010 and chose to go pro before graduating.
Professional sports: Arguably one of the most popular players in NFL
history, Rob moved to the Tampa Bay Buccaneers in 2020 after
a one-year hiatus. He played tight end for the New England
Patriots for 9 years, has been to 6 Super Bowls, earned 4 Super
Bowl rings, and has been named All Pro five times. Expected to
become Hall of Famer.
Today: Plays tight end for Tampa Bay Buccaneers where they won
Super Bowl LV in February 2021 and continues to light up the
internet with outrageous and charming antics and heartwarm-
ing community service. He was recently an on-air commentator
for Fox NFL and World Wrestling Entertainment (WWE), a
spokesman for CBD Oil and starred on the Masked Singer and
cohosted "Game On" with Venus Williams. He hosted Gronk
Beach before the Super Bowl in 2019, when he wasn't on the
field for a change, and joins his brothers in the traveling contest Stadium Blitz. Future plans might include small and big
screen as he has appeared in several TV shows and films and has
expressed a desire to do more. Lives in Foxborough, MA, and
Tampa, FL.

Glenn Gronkowski—"Goose," the baby, thoughtful, reserved
Born: March 25, 1993, Amherst, NY
Height: 6'3"
Weight: 245 lbs.
Birth weight: 8 lbs., 12 oz.
School: Kansas State University, double degree in management and
     marketing, minor in leadership.
Professional sports: Signed with the NFL Buffalo Bills in 2016, later
     that year was released and signed to the New England Patriots
     practice squad joining big brother Rob. Glenn also has a Super
     Bowl ring from the 2016 game. He played preseason in 2017
     for the Patriots but was released.
Today: Lives in Dallas and works for REVELXP.

Chris's wedding

WHEN EATING IS ALSO A CONTACT SPORT

Shopping list—Tuesday
Boneless chicken breasts—40 lbs.
Whole milk—7 gallons
Gatorade powdered mix—5 containers
Gallon freezer bags—6 boxes
Laundry soap—2 gallons
Half cow
Strawberries—10 quarts

I know there are people out there who studied for years to become a professional chef. They wear an apron with style as they cut tomatoes into perfect tiny cubes and decorate a cake to resemble a painting. There may be yelling in their kitchens along with sweating assistants and drawers full of special equipment. I don't have any of those things, though there may have been some yelling when food disappeared from the counter where I was working to get a completed meal on the table. I challenge any professional chef to chop and mix with one hand while swatting away thieving hands with the other.

I learned by osmosis how to handle forty pounds of raw chicken breasts at one time, enough milk to float a boat, and a single butcher order equivalent to half a cow. My mother was a stay-at-home mom, and one of my favorite things to do was hang out in the kitchen with her, cooking and baking for our family of eight, me being number four in the lineup of kids. Many of my recipes come from her and are fond memories of my own childhood, especially the super popular chicken soufflé. And she learned the same way I did, coming from a family of seven siblings. So, as far as training goes, I can't convert ounces to grams or make my own mayonnaise, but I can tell you how many quarts of fresh strawberries make a dozen jars of my homemade jam (forty) and how long a gallon of milk would last in my house (duration of one meal).

When I meet someone new and they discover my secret identity as mother to five professional athlete sons, the first thing they want to know is, how did I do it? By "it," they usually mean, how and what did I feed those boys? The answer is very simple: everything, anything, and always. I didn't have a big garbage can in my kitchen because I didn't need one. They ate everything.

My children were always hungry. From the time they could talk and open the refrigerator door, there was a constant chorus of "What can we eat?" As soon as they entered the house, I rarely heard "Hi, Mom" or "How was your day?" Instead, the usual greeting was "Mom! I'm starving!" It was a refrain that only quieted when their mouths were full. I was certain to hear it again less than a half hour after they had eaten a meal.

My young sons would complain dramatically, but they had no idea what starving really meant. Nor did they understand what it took to keep them fed, not that I would expect them to. They didn't even realize that some recipes called for more than one step. Chris would swoop through the kitchen and grab a cupcake that had just come from the oven, while Dan dug a spoon into the bowl of frosting on the counter, and Rob could shove an entire muffin into his mouth. Gordie was famous for asking his younger brothers, "Are you going to eat that?" and stealing a gigantic bite of whatever they held in their hands before they could answer.

Before they got to school age, my grocery-shopping expeditions were a cross between a circus act and a marathon. I would have two carts. In one, toddlers Dan and Chris sat in the child seats; infant Rob was in the baby carrier in the large section. The other cart was open for groceries, while biggest brother, Gordie, walked alongside, helping me keep the wheels straight as I stretched my arms past my pregnant belly where baby Glenn was kicking and ready to get out and join his brothers. Gordie was very serious about his job, and all small arms and legs were accounted for by the time we made it to the checkout line. Often, one of the boys would pick up forbidden things and drop them into the cart. Another would follow his brother's lead and do the same. But unlike those parents who loudly insist "No!" when their kids add a Snickers bar to the cart, I avoided the ear-piercing meltdown with a different game plan. I would nod and smile when my sons tossed sugary cereals and chocolate bars into the cart. When we got to the register, they were so busy jostling one another, looking at the rows of gum and candy on display at eye level and "helping" to put things on the conveyor belt, that they never noticed when I removed the offending items and quietly put them aside. Another trick I used to deflect the "wannas" was to allow each boy to choose one doughnut at the beginning of the shopping trip. Of course they all chose the messiest ones covered with sprinkles, but this kept them quiet and happy. I used the empty bag as a reminder to tell the cashier to add the cost to my total at the register. Today they are all health conscious and into fitness and have actually thanked me for not giving them soda and candy on a regular basis when they were young.

As the kids started going to school, one by one my grocery-shopping team was reduced to where finally I was alone. Without their grabby little hands and kicking feet, I could move unencumbered through the food-gathering ritual more quickly. This didn't last long because as they grew, the necessary volume of food increased dramatically. I always needed two carts, which I learned to manage quite easily minus a pregnant belly and small helpers.

I drove a huge, well-loved Ford conversion van in those days. It had extra seats and plenty of room for all the people and stuff I needed to move around. In my food-gathering rounds, I would stop at a local butcher that I went to for years. He was a jovial guy who knew me by name and was ready with my prepared order when I arrived at the shop. He would have four ten-pound packages of chicken, along with a half cow's worth of beef cut up and packaged to go straight into my freezer. Armed with a dozen boxes of zip top plastic bags, I'd spend the next few hours after I got home repacking the chicken for easier storage. I'd bake a few batches of cookies, do a few loads of laundry, and brace myself for the hour when the school bus brought home my afternoon tornado of boy energy.

When the boys were small, I tried to do at least one meal together as a family every day. Soon we were down to once a week, then sports took over our lives, and I just gave up altogether. With five sons, their increasingly complicated schedules, and a husband often away, it was simply impossible to have regular mealtimes. Plus, what was a regular mealtime anyway?

Because I bought so much food, a lot of it was frozen first, before it could be eaten for a snack or revolving meal. This practice may seem strange, but it was how I kept track of everything and maintained control of the flow. As my rambunctious team of boys grew and began to tower over me, I found that I needed two refrigerators, along with two freezers in the garage, to keep up with the demand and volume to supply it. And even that wasn't always enough room. I had to keep so much milk in the house (they drank it at every meal) that I'd often store reserve gallons in my neighbor's fridge too. I would cook forty hot dogs, hundreds of chicken nuggets, and several dozen hamburgers at one time, then put them in the freezer for later (and constant) consumption. This went for everything including French toast, meatballs, all the things I loved to bake—muffins, brownies, cookies, Texas sheet cake. My fridges and freezers looked like completed puzzles: everything stacked according to date, shape, and content. At one point, I switched to all clear storage containers so it was easy for everyone to determine what was inside. The guys pulled out what they wanted to eat when they wanted it. They were usually pretty good about making sure the rest was in place before they closed the door. Along with the refrigerator, that microwave was probably the hardest working appliance in my kitchen.

This orderliness wouldn't last too long. I remember standing in the laundry room, folding my third load of the day when I heard a tremendous crash, followed by raucous laughter. That's how it was in our house—too much noise or complete silence was always cause for suspicion. I ran into the kitchen and saw freezer containers all over the floor. The boys all stared up with a "Who me?" expression on their faces. I thought I would blow my top. Instead, I took five breaths and asked the nearest darling, "Chris, would you like to explain what happened?"

Son number three filled me in enthusiastically. A mysterious "someone" had stacked things up precariously in the freezer, slamming the door quickly so that the contents would come crashing down on the next person who opened it. Before I could choose a fitting response, Rob picked up a few frozen containers and attempted to juggle them. That was all it took to distract me from how mad I was, and I gave into laughter. Soon we were all laughing and I don't even remember who returned all those containers to the freezer. Probably me.

Green spoon

This is how it happened every time my team of exasperating troublemakers made me angry. Sometimes I would even chase them around, trying to seem threatening, with a green plastic spoon raised over my head. I rarely caught one of them, certainly never the culprit. Typically, it was Rob who diffused the tension with some silly comment or action, and he still plays this role in the family today. Their creativity and exuberance drove me crazy, but it would ultimately serve them well as ambitious problem solvers later in life.

Like so many young couples, Gordon Sr. and I didn't have much money when we first got married. Thankfully, I had good training for my job as frugal team mom for the Gronkowski family. In addition to all the meal management tricks she shared, my mother demonstrated that as a stay-at-home mom, she wasn't bringing money in, but she was not frivolously letting it go out either. A great example of that thriftiness is our family favorite, strawberry jam. When I was a kid, June was the wonderful time I shared with my mom and my sisters. We would spend all day picking (and eating) strawberries, then we would go home and make jam. We usually brought back thirty to forty quarts of berries. After removing the stems, we would wash and crush the fruit, add sugar and pectin, and let the mixture sit on the counter for twenty-four hours. From there, the jam went into plastic or glass containers and into the freezer. We also made strawberry pies, but they didn't last very long, so there was no need to freeze those. At that moment in my life, I had no idea how important that jam would be to my little boys and the huge men they would become. To this day, they ask me to bring it with me when I come to visit.

My mom also taught me to bake. When I was a teenager, I was pretty shy and often lonely on account of the frequent moves my family made. I joined the basketball team in high school to make friends, but I didn't have the passion for sports that my boys have. Baking with my mom became a lifelong form of relaxation and a coping mechanism when stress threatened to slow me down. As a mom myself, I especially enjoyed the ritual of baking during the day while the house was quiet. I loved even more the joyful consumption when the boys came home from school. My chocolate chip cookies aren't from a special recipe, and I certainly won't win any art contest with them, but for some reason, that was a very popular request. I think years and years of practice, filling the cookie plate as fast as it was emptied, has made my cookies special.

Not only was it important to get good deals on the prices of food I needed for the family; it was my form of fun. I have to admit that I really liked the hunt for a bargain, and I still do. I had the luxury of extra storage to accommodate the irresistible deals I'd happen on. When I passed a convenience store advertising two-for-one gallons of ice cream, I'd swing my van around and clear out their inventory. This way, the kids could have a treat and it wouldn't completely empty out my wallet.

By the time all the boys were in school, we got into a surprisingly manageable meal routine. We had mornings down to a simple, streamlined process: orange juice and cold cereal with milk on weekdays, pancakes and French toast with bacon and sausage as a treat on the weekends.

School lunches were also very simple, predictable, and generally acceptable to all. Everyone got two lunches (one for midday, one for right after school) consisting of peanut butter and homemade strawberry jam sandwiches, fruit, homemade cookies, and two frozen bottles of Gatorade, which they dutifully brought home empty each evening. I would wash out the bottles, refill with Gatorade I made from the powdered mix to save money, then put them into the freezer for the next day. Ten bottles. Every day. I saved a lot of aggravation by avoiding personal tastes (thankfully, no allergies) like who wouldn't eat mayonnaise and who didn't like cheese. Same thing every day, no complaints—at least not that they dared let me hear.

For dinners, we usually had some sort of casserole or lasagna. Every week, the menu rotation featured the family favorite, chicken soufflé. This is a recipe from my mom and something that my siblings and I always loved when we were kids. It is not a soufflé really, but more of a classic chicken casserole with vegetables, cream of chicken soup, chopped chicken breast and of course, lots of love. I made the casseroles at night when the kids were in bed (rarely sleeping) and put them in the freezer for the week. To this day I believe that chicken soufflé could be the secret to the success of my boys. I always had a hot dish of this favorite waiting in the car as we went from one practice to another. I didn't believe in fast-food so this was a great way for me to control what they consumed and it helped me keep the budget in line.

My life was nonstop cooking and I'm sure I dreamed of going out to eat now and then, but the reality of a restaurant meal, along with the expense of hiring a babysitter, was in fact not worth the effort. Not only was it costly, but can you imagine taking five young boys to a restaurant? I must admit, I did take them out a few times, not as a form of self-torture, but to teach them how to behave in public. Despite their obvious charms on the playing field and their darned good grades in school, I feel we all need to learn a few of the social graces to make it in the world. (Which they did. Eventually. I think?)

On rare occasions we would go out for a meal. One of the family's favorite places to eat out was Denny's and this was also one of the few places that wouldn't break the bank. I had more than my hands full getting all five boys to sit nicely and stop moving and provoking each other. And that was just in the car on the way to the restaurant. I would use my stern mom voice, "If you don't behave, I'll turn this car around and go straight home." But who was I kidding? I was the one who would lose in that equation, because if we turned around and went straight home then I'd be the one who was cooking and cleaning up, not the nice folks at Denny's. Once in a while, I actually had to turn that car around and nobody was happy about that.

Once we got into the restaurant and were escorted to our table, the gang of five played musical chairs, jockeying for whatever position was most desired by someone else. Sugar packets and saltshakers were rearranged. Menus were held upside down to see who could read the fastest. Truly, every single moment of every day was a competition. We always got the $1.99 breakfast special and except for the constant stealing of each other's orange juice, this worked out great. For a while. Soon, their oversized appetites matched their growing bodies and we were getting two breakfasts for each son. You would not believe the number of plates and glasses covering the table by the time we were done. That was definitely a thanksgiving moment for me: I was thankful that I didn't have to deal with all of those dishes.

For the same reason a meal at a restaurant resembled a WWE event, we were rarely welcomed into people's homes for dinner. Once Gordy Sr. and I were invited to a "grown-ups only" Super Bowl party only to discover there were children there—all girls. This was surprising and hurtful to me. Message received. It became apparent that if we weren't going to be invited to other people's parties, the boys would have to bring the social life to our house. This meant meals at home, lots of guests and the constant challenge of keeping food on the table. But I really didn't mind. The atmosphere was always lively, and most importantly, I got to know who my sons were hanging around with. The ultimate goal of the watchful parent, knowing your kids' friends, is not always easy to achieve. I learned a lot from overheard conversations delivered through mouthfuls of burgers and cookies.

Christmas with 5 boys & Dustin & Dylan

And so, from very early on my sons created their own fraternity with a membership of five plus two dogs, continually adding members in the form of classmates and teammates who came through the house and into the kitchen especially. Some came daily, some weekly, a few even stayed for years. If a kid came to the house looking to play with Dan, but Dan wasn't home, that kid would just stay and play with Chris and Rob. Their gregarious natures served them well. When Gordie played first base on the Little League team in Amherst, NY, I called him the mayor of the Lou Gehrig baseball complex because he got along so easily with everyone, including the opposing team members. I would count the number of boys who made it to first base during the game and that was the number of guys I could expect him to invite home for dinner that night. They all loved that chicken soufflé and asked for it day and night. I made a lot of it. I made it in my sleep. Even years later when most of the boys were out of the house, whoever came by still requested chicken soufflé and some wanted it mailed to them, an impossible wish to fulfill.

I went to visit Rob at his house in Foxborough, MA just before the New England Patriots 2017 pre-season training camp. Youngest son Glenn was living there too as he was also on the Patriots' roster at that time. I had never seen them play pre-season and I was really excited to be there. When I peeked into the refrigerator in the kitchen (of course there is one in the garage too), I saw a few energy drinks, the remains of a gallon of milk and leftovers in Styrofoam containers. Anticipating this, I had stopped at the grocery store on my way in from the airport to pick up some provisions so I could make their favorites.

Rob came through the door first yelling, "Mom! I'm home!" with a huge smile. That man can fill a room for sure. Behind him, my shy Glenn followed, laughing at his brother. I was engulfed in a group hug and both asked at the same time, "Is there chicken soufflé?" Not five minutes together! I gave them homemade strawberry jam that I'd brought on the plane, so they could have PB&J for an appetizer poolside while they relaxed after practice, as I cooked their favorite meal. It was a beautiful day and every few minutes one of them would pop his head into the kitchen to ask when the soufflé would be ready. I rarely feel as happy as times like this.

Looking back, I realize that the constant in my life is food. Thinking about food, budgeting, shopping, cooking, cleaning up food. It also meant watching with great pleasure while my five boys enjoyed their meals as they grew bigger and stronger right before my eyes. Even when I worked at Wegman's grocery store, I was cooking in the prepared foods department making 150 entrées at a time.

Being a mother to young children means rarely finding time for yourself. People have asked me how I did it. Well, I would counter with my own question: How could I not? I couldn't send the kids back, though there were days when I would have loved to. I did it because I love my sons fiercely. And I did it because watching a hungry child light up with pleasure when eating food that I prepared makes me happier than anything I could ever do for myself.

"MAMA GRONK SAYS..."

1. Planning is essential to survival in the kitchen. Plan ahead. Plan way ahead if you can. While it may feel like you have no time to sit down and make a list, you will actually gain time if you take a few minutes at the beginning of the week (I liked Sunday nights) to look at the calendar and plan the meals for every day. This accomplishes two things: you create a shopping list that makes sense and avoid buying unnecessary items; you are mindful of exactly how many veggies, fruits, and healthy snacks you'll have ready, so there is no panicky throwing a bag of potato chips at the kids when they say they are hungry and you are running ten minutes late because someone couldn't find their science notebook. Unless, of course, you are in the mood for potato chips. It is a completely different story when you are experiencing panic hunger yourself.

2. There is no shame in cheating. Buy frozen, chopped onion, cut-up celery and carrots, shredded cheese. Take advantage of a sale and put a package or two in the freezer for future use. Anything that helps you get dinner on the table and has no consequence to nutrition and taste, go ahead and cheat. Absolutely no one will know (or care) if you chopped those tomatoes yourself or made the bread crumbs in your food processor. A word of caution: read the labels on prepared foods carefully. There can be a lot of salt and sugar hiding there.

3. The freezer is your best friend. Honest! You can take advantage of great deals at the grocery store (think two for one times ten). Online shopping has transformed the way we can buy food— Google for bargains and coupons. Don't forget warehouse stores

like Costco, Sam's Club, local food cooperatives. You can get dozens of muffins into a dozen boxes of zip top bags, place in the freezer and you've got breakfast or snacks covered for a month— or a week, depending on the size and appetite of your crew. The same goes for boneless chicken, burgers, steaks, pork chops, hot dogs; anything you buy in bulk can be broken into smaller portions. It is important to label and date each bag (include heating/defrosting instructions). My favorite trick is to cook those things before freezing, making it super easy for the kids to just take out of the freezer and zap in the microwave. You can even freeze milk, cheese, butter, and little plastic yogurt pots. Big bags of frozen vegetables are especially useful in winter months when fresh produce is at its highest price. Make cupcakes for that birthday party two weeks from now. All you need to do is defrost, make frosting, and sprinkle with jimmies.

4. Don't give them choices. Make common foods, like a favorite casserole or meal elements that the family can customize. For example, you know everyone loves mashed potatoes; make a lot of that and offer broccoli and carrots without fancy sauces or complicated preparation. They won't complain because it is much easier to consume mass quantities of something already on the table than it is to make such things for themselves. One meal for dinner for the whole family at one general time. You are not a short-order cook. And if you don't act like one, they won't expect you to be.

5. KISS—keep it simple, sweetheart. Don't make things harder than they already are. Prepare simple recipes without fancy presentation. No one at your table appreciates a decorative carrot flower, sprig of parsley, or swirl of balsamic vinegar reduction. Your crew will likely have inhaled the meal in front of them long before they think much about what was actually on the plate in the first place. Do yourself a favor, save the gourmet stuff for when they are all away at college.

6. Tools for success. Make sure you have the proper tools to do the work. Big bowls, food processor, mixer, blender, spoons, spatulas, knives. Don't be afraid to use these things to achieve the

gigantic results you need to keep your team fueled for all they do. Don't worry about using as many of these tools as necessary. This is why God made dishwashers.

7. Ask your army for help. It is never too early to enlist the aid of your small warriors in taking care of the important ritual of food prep and cleanup. One can load the dishwasher, another can microwave the already-cooked bacon from the freezer, someone else can be in charge of the toaster. Don't forget your four-legged teammates as they are excellent at floor cleaning and crumb control.

8. Give yourself a break and don't worry about the mess. One big, thorough cleaning of the kitchen each day is really all you need. I like to do it at the end of the day. A good friend leaves it all overnight and starts fresh by cleaning up in the morning. Personal choice! Of course, it is necessary to tackle big spills right away and put away uneaten food (if there is any). Besides that, no one is going to judge you on the "perfection" of your kitchen.

MAMA GRONK'S FAMOUS CHICKEN SOUFFLÉ

(serves 8 or 4 *really* hungry teenagers)

8 slices of white or wheat
     bread, cubed
4 cups cooked, diced chicken
1 cup chopped celery
1 large white onion, chopped
1/2 cup mayo or Miracle
     Whip (I use Miracle
     Whip Light)
3 cups milk
4 eggs
1 can condensed cream of
     mushroom soup (I use
     Campbells)
3 cups grated cheddar cheese
     (use more or less to taste)

Chicken Soufflé recipe

Grease bottom of 9×13 pan. Line with 4 slices of cubed bread. Combine chicken, celery, onion, and mayo and spread over bread. Cover chicken mixture with the next 4 slices of cubed bread. Combine egg with milk and pour over top. Cover and let sit in refrigerator for several hours or overnight. Remove cover and bake for approximately 1 hour at 350°F, checking that the center is firm. Remove from oven, spread can of cream of mushroom soup on top, and then sprinkle the cheddar cheese on top of soup. Bake another 5–10 minutes, to melt cheese. Casserole will have puffed up, like a soufflé.

Tips: You could buy the onion and celery already chopped from the produce department or buy frozen onion. If you have leftover chicken from another meal, especially rotisserie chicken, cut it up and put it in the freezer for when you want to make the chicken soufflé recipe. Cooked soufflé can be frozen but may "deflate."

25

EARMUFFS CAN BE A FASHION STATEMENT

Earmuffs
Blanket (for me)
Bucket of pucks
Hockey sticks (in van)
Water and snacks (inside house, so as not to freeze)
Gigantic gear bags (also inside) including, but not limited to,
skates, helmets, shin guards, socks, shoulder and elbow pads,
jerseys, gloves, neck guards, and most importantly, weiner cups

Hockey is where my kids caught sports fever, and this is where I began my long and varied career in managing everybody's everything. What started as one little boy, age six, expressing a desire to play hockey with his friends morphed into a round-the-clock job of shuttling five children across town multiple times per day, bringing food, dry clothes, homework, backpacks, huge gear bags, and the occasional friend.

Over time, the number and distance of the trips increased and the elapsed hours spread from 4:00 a.m. to midnight, even on Sundays. Hockey season slid into basketball season, overlapping with baseball season then immediately into preseason football training. In between the major sports, all five boys enjoyed golf, volleyball, snow skiing, and just about anything else involving a ball, running, and competition.

Somewhere around midnight on the night before our very first ice hockey experience, I crawled into bed next to my snoring husband. I'm wearing the very sexy lingerie of a brand-new hockey mom: sweatpants and a turtleneck. My heavy socks, a sweater, and gloves are piled neatly on the floor next to the bed. It is permanently cold in Buffalo, so I am actually glad to go to bed fully dressed.

It feels like I have only just closed my eyes when the alarm goes off. It is 4:00 a.m., and I'm already ahead of the game as I climb out of bed and scoop up my things from the floor. Silently, I creep out of the room and work my way down the hall, waking the first of four young boys to play hockey that day. That first year, the sleeping baby would stay home with his sleeping dad. I will make hundreds of round trips to the rinks in the following years as the schedules change, rinks get farther away, and other activities are thrown into the mix.

On this particular morning, the boys emerge from bedrooms, though not necessarily their own. So often I find one in another's room, or all of them together in one bedroom, having slept wherever they landed. Occasionally, I have even woken the wrong kid because he was not in the right bed. They just seem to go to sleep wherever they are at that particular time of their day. They look sleepy and tousled, but definitely ready to roll. My boys have also slept in their clothes; pajamas seem to be so frivolous. This saves precious time as we have about thirty minutes to eat, gather gear, load the van, and get to the rink for their 4:50 a.m. ice time. The earlier hours are reserved for the younger kids. Ice time is less expensive than later in the day and usually available.

It is so dark and quiet on those early mornings as I drive my unusually subdued crew through town to the hockey rink complex. The only people out on the road with me are the town snowplows and delivery trucks. It is really eerie and peaceful at the same time.

Who would want to get up at such an ungodly hour to do this? I wondered. When six-year-old Gordie said he wanted to play hockey, I said okay, not realizing how early it would be. At that time, Dan was five, Chris was three, and Rob just one year old. I don't mind getting up early, but as the kids started to join their older brother, it became quite a challenge to juggle children, their schedules, and their stuff. Of course, I did not know it at the time, but this was the beginning of sports careers that would span decades, take over the entire family, and set the stage for future greatness for all five of my sleepy boys. For me, it was also the first of hundreds of early mornings, frozen feet, and hours and hours spent shuttling young people to sports fields all across New York state and, eventually, the country.

The first time I put on my earmuffs, it was not just to keep warm. I had to do something with my hair—I barely had time to brush my teeth on those black, early mornings. This was a fashion statement that would carry me through many seasons.

At that time, I knew absolutely nothing about hockey or the equipment. We got to the rink early that first day. None of the other players or coaches had arrived yet. I had bought a hockey bag and all of the gear on the list handed out by the coaches. We were ready. Except for the skates and the jockstrap, I had no idea how the rest of it went on.

Gordie was so excited, and finally, another player arrived with his dad. I watched how he got his son dressed, and I followed along, getting the shoulder pads and neck guard into position, socks with shin guards facing the right direction. I'll never forget my son's brown eyes shining in happiness as I fastened the chin strap on his helmet. We popped the mouth guard in, and he was off. My little warrior.

One by one, the younger Gronkowskis followed their big brother onto the ice. In the early days, it was the same experience for each one: the small players would just fly around the ice, screaming in excitement and joyously using their sticks to slap at the puck and each other. Most of those little boys were sopping wet from spending more time flat out on the ice than gliding along, upright, on their skates.

The team would come off the ice and shout, "Did we win?" I always said yes, even if the score was really a loss of 20 to 1. They didn't care about the score or blue lines or offsides. They were so happy, and all they really wanted to know was who brought the snacks and when they could eat.

The subject of snacks was always top of mind in our family. One particular challenge we faced at the hockey rink was the siren call of the vending machines. There was a huge foyer in the center of the rink complex. It was lined with benches and vending machines displaying all kinds of sodas, candy, chips—you name it. It became clear to me that I didn't want to manage so much loose change and various requests for this sugary drink or those cheesy crackers, so I gave each boy ten dollars at the beginning of the season to use as he wished. They could blow it all on candy the first day, or they could save the money and bring snacks from home. I know it is hard to believe, but none of them had trouble making this choice. They all became savers, and I think they quickly figured out they could bring a lot more from home. Remember, my sons were always hungry.

The boys really did a lot of self-policing. Sure, they would do things that would make me angry, but more often than not, we ended up laughing at something Rob did to distract us and the incident would be over. Punishment might be extra chores such as cleaning their bedrooms or emptying the dishwasher. I never demanded that they make their beds or do regularly assigned jobs because they were all very good about doing homework and generally cooperating and staying out of trouble. Of course, there must be plenty of things contrary to this statement, but at the moment, I am blissfully unaware. To me, their job was doing well in school, after-school activities, and sports. Besides, I found any punishment I might give them, such as having to stay in their rooms, was more punishing for me. Somebody had to stay home and enforce the punishment, and I sure didn't like it as much as they didn't like it.

They would wrestle and beat up on each other, but not to the point of serious injury. Bruises and bumps were part of the family uniform at our house, no matter what sports season we were in. Glenn, the youngest, is the only one to end up in the emergency room because of a roughhousing accident, but this was only because he got in the way when the bigger boys were settling their differences. The older boys were closest in age and became a team, while the youngest was treated with a little more respect as he really was much smaller than they were. At least at the beginning.

The boys didn't tell on one another to me or their dad; they just figured things out for themselves. They operated in their own, self-policing bubble. If things got too intense (say, between Chris and

Dan), Rob would do something goofy and distract everyone. Instead of escalating a minor altercation into an all-out brawl (which also happened), the whole bunch would be laughing and forgetting what the fight was about in the first place. It's funny, Rob and Glenn joke around like that today, as grown men. They crack me up by saying in a loud, whiny voice, "Mom! He touched my shirt!" That just wasn't a thing when they were young.

As my budding fraternity got older, they continued to play hockey and joined travel teams. This made those early morning schedules fluctuate wildly. Usually, there were two brothers on one team at a time, which was a big help. I would get up early, take one or two to the rink, then double back to the house to pick up whoever was next on the ice, take him to the rink, and pick up the first two and get them home for some breakfast, and their turn at the newspaper delivery route they shared.

One week, Gordie and Chris delivered the papers while Dan was on the ice. Another week, Dan and Rob would deliver the papers while Chris was on the ice. Of course, there was the expected squabbling over what could be deemed "fair," but they were very happy to get that pocket money. They split the proceeds from each week, depending on who was working, and most of the money they earned went directly into their bank accounts. The boys delivered papers on Saturday and Sunday mornings and after school during the week. They delivered the neighborhood papers on foot or bike, and I drove them to the customers who lived farther away. I always drove them in bad weather and on Sundays when the newspapers were so heavy. There were at least 130 papers to be delivered; you just couldn't carry many at one time.

When Glenn, the youngest, was only five days old, seven-year-old Dan's hockey team made it to the championships. I got a babysitter that day, but for the rest of the time, that baby went everywhere we did.

It was certainly interesting crossing the dark huge ice rink parking lot in those early hours with five kids in tow. I would have a diaper bag over one shoulder, a hockey bag over the other, push the stroller, and hold as many hands as I could. I developed excellent balance, which I put to good use in the locker room as we juggled the bags and the boys and managed to get everyone dressed and ready for practice.

I would sit at the top of the bleachers using the wall to support my tired back and to keep our stuff together. While one brother (or two) was on the ice, the others would stay with me and play in the stands, sometimes with other waiting siblings of kids on the ice. I was permanently armed with snacks, toys, balls, and wet wipes. My hands would bleed from pulling on skate laces in the freezing cold, and I sure treasured that blanket I sat on.

Later, the schedule would include travel to other rinks, and I would take my turn driving other players to compete against distant teams. Depending on their age groups, games could be hours away from home and from each other. When they reached age twelve or so, I finally felt that I could relax enough to trust another parent to drive them. Of course, I was happy to take other kids, but it was harder for me to let mine go in another car. The schedules got so crazy that eventually I had no choice, and obviously, everyone survived. They played in Canada, Pittsburgh, Rochester, Syracuse, and Erie, PA. Even on Sunday afternoons, we would be going from one rink to another. Sometimes, 5:00 p.m. felt like midnight to me. Hockey was so time-consuming that I was glad when the boys finally got into high school sports and things like travel were out of my hands.

My boys really loved hockey and skated all through their teens. At the same time, they were adding basketball, baseball, tennis, golf, and football to their repertoire. Dan was the only one to play hockey in high school. Glenn, the youngest who couldn't wait to join his brothers on the ice, ended up not liking hockey as much as the rest of them. I know he just didn't want to get up that early, and he still doesn't.

I ran a pretty tight ship. I had to. It began with Gordie when our dining room table became hockey central. We had our routines; as they got older, the guys were responsible for their gear bags, getting jerseys out of the clean laundry basket, making sure everything was in its place and ready for the next practice. They just followed the drill, I think because they loved the game so much. Being a stay-at-home mom was essential to my sanity and their success as sports began to take over our lives. I was there when they came home; I was there in the morning to get them out the door. I knew where they were and what they were up to. I could not and would not have been happy to spend my time doing anything else.

At the end of the day, when most parents would sit down to watch TV, I emptied the hockey bags of stinky jerseys into the washing machine. This special scent I refer to as "the stench." I'd get a casserole in the oven, set the bath ritual in motion, feed the boys in shifts, get them ready for bed, do the dishes, set the alarm, and fall into bed. Repeat.

BASEBALL BRINGS OUT THE BEST IN ALL OF US

Socks—dozen pair
Snacks—no chocolate
Sunscreen
Baseball bats—plastic, wood, metal
Baby-food jars—banana

They say diamonds are a girl's best friend, and I'll tell you, I'm not that kind of girl. I will say, however, that despite our reputation as a football family, baseball diamonds have been an important part of my mom life for decades. From the end of hockey to the beginning of basketball, America's pastime became our family obsession. All my boys spent their days from April to August on one of the ten baseball fields in the Lou Gehrig complex in Amherst, New York, and they could not have been happier.

Our baseball days were long ones. We would get there early and often stay past dark. It was especially exciting when one of the boys got to play under the lights. I can only imagine what it must have looked like when the Gronkowskis arrived. Me struggling to push the overloaded stroller through the heavy gravel on the pathway (later paved when my baby was able to walk and didn't need a stroller anymore) with four boys running ahead, excited and proud in their uniforms. I had my usual spot where I would set up camp—a perfect location to monitor the action on all the fields. I wouldn't want to miss one of my guys at bat. You would think my spot would be near the restrooms, but in the early days, they only had outhouses. No thank you! I managed to take the smallest ones with me and sneak home for a brief comfort break. Thank God they installed toilets at the ballfields when they updated the concession stand.

Lou Gehrig Baseball (5 Boys)

The kids had a lot of freedom at that complex. In between their games, they would run around with their friends (maybe five hundred kids on a Saturday afternoon), checking out other games and just enjoying the ability to go off on their own. They got ice cream and came back to me every so often, sometimes with a scraped knee, sometimes for a snack, and sometimes just to see if I was still there.

There was a gigantic dirt pile near my outpost which was a favorite place to play for any siblings not otherwise engaged in a game or practice. This was especially true for young Glenn, who wore a bicycle helmet when riding his push car for protection in the case of an errant pop fly. The activity on the dirt mound surely intensified when our tribe showed up. I allowed the boys to play there wearing only socks. This saved me from the tedious task of cleaning so many pairs of sneakers. When we got home, the socks went directly into the garbage and the boys went directly into the tub. That water was black and gritty by the time they were done, but boy did they have a good time.

Biggest brother Gordie was the first to catch baseball fever, and he never recovered. He played through high school and college and was drafted by the Los Angeles Angels for their farm team. Throughout his life, Gordie played many sports in the off-season, but baseball was his first and steadfast love.

Not surprisingly, the rest of the crew followed suit and played various positions, occasionally coached by their dad. As they moved up in the league, each one became an umpire and earned some very good money for spending time on the fields that they wanted to be at anyway. They were always going to each other's games and brought their ump gear just in case there was a no-show providing an opportunity for one of them to call the game. I know Rob enjoyed his time as an umpire and took special delight in calling a strike on his younger brother before the ball even left the pitcher's hand. Always the joker, he was kidding of course. I know they all took that job seriously and did their best to be fair and accurate. The boys did not have after-school jobs because their sports schedules were so packed, so this was a perfect situation for all of them. They learned the responsibility of having a job but still managed to maintain their crazy sports schedules.

Between Little League and travel teams, my boys hit an all-time high of being on thirteen teams at once. That meant thirteen uniforms to be washed and ready for between ten and fifteen games each week. Add in practices and you've got a lot of baseball to manage. And that is why I loved the concession stand.

This is the one place I relaxed my meal standards a bit. The entire complex was run by volunteers, so I did my time working in that concession stand, sometimes at the grill, sometimes scooping ice cream. The prices were great as most things were sold at cost. I knew the quality of the food was good because of my involvement there. I think I loved it even more than my kids did. For me, a heavenly meal was simple: I did not have to plan it, buy it, cook it, or clean up. They had the usual burgers, hot dogs, fries, watermelon, ice cream, and homemade goodies brought by a rotating army of mostly mom volunteers. You could get a whole meal, called the Grand Slam, for $2.50, including a hot dog or hamburger, fries, and a drink. You just could not go wrong, and every Gronkowski was happy.

Every July 4, there was a daylong baseball jamboree, so we didn't celebrate the holiday at home. We did, however, host quite a few team parties at our house because we had the pool and a big backyard. I think the kids really enjoyed those parties. I sure did. Yes, it was a lot of work, but it was so much fun. Those parties were always planned last-minute. The tournament would end at 5:00 p.m., and parents would start talking about what to do after the game. Everyone would go home to get swimsuits and pick up chips, beer, sodas. I was famous for having a well-stocked freezer full of hot dogs and rolls, so everyone would just bring something to go with it, potluck style.

Gordie & Diane

I continued to enjoy going to Gordie's games when he went to college and when he hopped around to various minor league teams. We talked on the phone every day when he was on the road. This is where he developed a taste for the banana baby food. I guess it was like the goop you see lots of current athletes squeezing into their mouths for energy during a game. He played in Utah, Ohio, Illinois, Pennsylvania, Arizona, Connecticut, Montana, and in a tournament on Cape Cod in Massachusetts. The players would share hotel rooms or stay with local families for the season. When he played for the Orem Owls, in Utah, he stayed with a family with two young kids, which he really enjoyed. This was not a big budget operation, but the atmosphere around those teams was relaxed and friendly. I just loved watching Gordie signing autographs and posing for pictures after every game. He stayed until the last fan got their autograph or shook his hand. Those fans just loved him. I wonder why he is not coaching now as he was always so good with his younger brothers, his fellow players, and those kids waiting for him to come off the field.

Despite my years and years facing the cold of hockey and the crazy crowds of football, I will admit that I just loved baseball. It was not a hardship for me to sit at that complex for hours, relaxing on a sunny day.

I don't really follow baseball anymore. I don't have a favorite team, though my husband, Mike, and I enjoy going to see the minor-league Mussels play in Fort Myers every once in a while. I would consider hosting a player just as some wonderful people hosted my son. It's funny how something can consume your entire life for a period of time, and then it's gone. This is a lot like motherhood, I guess.

Everything was a competition when my boys were growing up. It used to drive me crazy when they just had to see who could fling the most spitballs, eat the most cookies, or toss the most basketball free throws. Somehow the competition did not turn ugly; it just seemed to motivate them. I do feel like the luckiest mom when it comes to that. And whenever there was trouble for one Gronkowski brother, it became a problem for all the Gronkowski brothers. All for one and one for all!

Hockey season would morph into basketball season, but once that moved into baseball season, you could still find my boys shooting hoops. They just loved to play, and they still do. They played in the driveway, they played in the basement, they played in the pool.

They tried to play basketball in the living room, but that is where I drew the line. Coach Mom called foul on that one.

They still play basketball today. At Rob's home in Boston, there is a gigantic basketball court just beyond the in-ground swimming pool, which also has a basketball net and backboard installed. While swimming in the pool, there is constant hoop shooting, which inevitably evolves into a competition. Everything with these guys is, and always has been, a competition.

HAVE CONVERSION VAN WILL TRAVEL

Wash and vacuum the van
Tommee Tippee cup
Goldfish crackers
Dumb & Dumber video
Peanut M&Ms
Marshall Tucker Band CD

We didn't get a lot of invitations to dinner at the neighbors' house or even to visit our family living nearby. I know it was just a lot to have us there—so much action, so much noise. That's okay. I understood. And when we did finally go on the road, I did my best to make it fun for all of us.

One place my crazy crew was welcomed with open arms was my parents' place on Rushford Lake, south of our Buffalo home. It took us about an hour and a half to get there, and I'll say it was a really great time for my kids but more than a little stressful for me. With the baseball schedule, it was hard to fit in these trips, but once in a while, I liked the kids to do things that weren't scheduled sporting events. We would go maybe half a dozen times each summer and just for the day because the boys had the paper route the next morning.

All my boys learned to water-ski and rode in an inflated tube behind the boat driven by my dad. They loved to fish and could stand on the dock to cast away to their hearts' content. I would have them put on their life vests before they got out of the van. Those vests stayed on their bodies until we left after dinner. They wore them to fish, swim, take a nap, and eat. It was hard for me to watch them all at the same time, so this worked for all of us. They learned that this was the way it was, and they just did it. Like kids with seat belts now, they don't know any different, so they just buckle up when they get in a vehicle. The boys never went to Rushford Lake without me.

I spent all my summers at that lake house as a kid, and the place

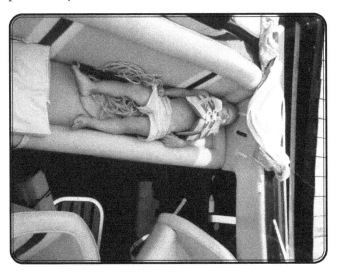

Chris with life vest on

holds wonderful memories for me. But when you put me into the role of mom in charge of five very active boys, my lovely memories fade a bit. When we pulled into the driveway, all my sons would hop out of the van, run right through the front door, directly out the back door and onto the dock. They would be permanently outside—fishing with my dad, water-skiing, swimming, throwing balls to one another and at one another. They were in constant motion and so very happy to be there. I remember one time, somebody pulled a drainpipe right off the house. I was horrified and ended up just taking them home. My parents laugh now, but at the time it wasn't so funny. I guess it was hard for me to remember that my parents were parents of a large family too. Just not nearly as rowdy.

Another family visit puts Rob at the center of the chaos. We had driven five hours to see my oldest brother in Connecticut, and by the time we stopped the car in his driveway, those boys were ready to get *out* and have fun with their cousins. Rob was so excited that he actually forgot to open the screen door and just plowed right through it. He only paused, then continued on his way as my brother and I stared at the door, completely off the hinges. My brother laughed, shrugged his shoulders, and fixed the darn thing.

Myrtle Beach

When the boys were small, before sports dictated our schedule, I tried to recreate a favorite childhood memory of my own family road trips but found it surprisingly challenging. Every Easter, when I was a child, we went to Myrtle Beach, South Carolina, for a week, driving sixteen hours straight through from our home in Buffalo, New York. There were nine of us in the station wagon, including my oldest brother's girlfriend. In those days, seat belts were not installed in most cars, and we lay out in the back like a can of sardines. Luggage was not a problem as we did not have any: everyone got one brown paper grocery bag to fill with the clothes and things they wanted for the week which my dad would then smush into the cartop carrier. We would leave in the evening, watching gray, cold, snowy Buffalo recede in the rearview mirror. I stayed awake all night, sitting between my parents in the front seat, feeding my dad grapes and Cheez Whiz on crackers. I loved to keep him company while he drove. By the time we arrived the next morning, it was warm and sunny and the air smelled deliciously of green trees and moss and the ocean. We stayed at a little hotel right on the beach. It had an unheated, outdoor pool and a kitchenette where my mom made most of our meals. We always brought gigantic coolers to supply this endeavor. She did all the meals except for the doughnuts we loved on Easter morning and one restaurant dinner out. These are such happy memories for me.

When I became a mom myself, I tried to make this same trip for my own kids. It sure was a lot harder to do than I thought it would be! My parents made it look easy.

So, when it was my turn to get behind the wheel of the family vehicle to drive through the night from cold Buffalo to warm Myrtle Beach, things were certainly a lot different. First, we had a video player in my large conversion van, which I certainly did not have as a kid, of course. My boys just watched Dumb & Dumber over and over. They would laugh at the same things every time, and I feel like I could recite the whole movie. On my watch, we had snacks, but nothing chocolate and melty. Except for me: I had my own stash of peanut M&Ms in the front seat. Call it Mom Privilege. I also had Marshall Tucker on the sound system to keep me company.

My tribe really didn't need games in the car; they entertained one another. But I was firm about the "no balls in the car" rule. I learned this the hard way when Rob was a toddler in a car seat. He threw a hockey puck trying to kill a bug and clocked me in the head instead.

We had our Tommee Tippee cup for in-between potty stops. Even this became a competition to see who could fill it the highest. I found out years later that the fraternity competition extended to whizzing out the car windows as well. Never a dull moment.

This was a sweet time for me, when they were small. The Easter bunny would come early to our house, the night before we left, and the boys would each get a sand pail as his Easter basket. In each, I would put a puzzle, a book, a few snacks, and just one piece of chocolate. It was Easter after all.

As the guys got older, the cooler we traveled with got bigger and the snacks became real meals. Chicken soufflé and lasagna were top favorites as we turned their sports travel into mini family vacations. I really enjoyed those road trips and the camaraderie with their teammates' families.

When Gordie was sixteen, the Little League World series was held in Burlington, Iowa. The whole family went, and we drove twelve hours from Buffalo. The players stayed with local families, the rest of us in budget hotels. I remember Gordie and a teammate stayed with an older couple one year. They had a pond on their property, so the boys fished. It was a quiet little town, so there wasn't much do to, but everyone was so nice. All the arrangements were made for the families: hotel rooms blocked off, restaurants and local entertainment reserved. We didn't see the players too much off the field because they were supposed to be resting in between games.

The spring high school baseball trips were more work. We had to do all our own planning, which was tough because all the Florida hotels were usually booked as this was a popular spring break time. We drove to St. Petersburg from Buffalo, and this didn't end up being the mini-vacation I would have liked it to be. The players had curfew, could not enjoy the hotel pool, and had to stay in their own rooms. We really didn't get much time together, and the game schedule prevented us from doing much else.

The shift from high school sports to college events helped me reach my career high of covering approximately five hundred thousand miles, eighteen states, and two countries. My butt remembers every mile. Back and forth to Gordie in college in Florida; Dan and Chris, in Maryland. Thankfully, we didn't drive to Arizona for Rob (then Chris) or Kansas for Glenn. This is why God made airplanes. There were no direct flights, so we still had to drive or take a bus two hours from Phoenix or make a Las Vegas connection to Tucson. Getting to Kansas was two flights and a two-hour drive.

Diane & Dan

Going pro in the NFL didn't mean that my driving days were over, far from it. Dan was drafted by the Detroit Lions in 2009, right out of college, but he wasn't old enough to rent a moving truck to get his belongings from Maryland to Michigan by way of Buffalo, New York. By that time, I was divorced from the boys' dad, so I went by myself to rent the truck and help Dan and his buddy load it with four years' worth of furniture, clothes, and God knows what. We drove 7 hours, nearly 450 miles to drop off the unneeded stuff into my living room for storage, a neat interior-decorating trick. From Buffalo, Dan flew to Detroit with what he needed in a couple of suitcases. Later, when he was traded to Denver, the NFL paid to move him. This was lucky because when a player is released and then picked up by another team, the NFL does not foot the bill. And it's up to the player (and his family) to move from city to city. Sometimes the guys will just stay in a hotel if they think their time will be short in one place, thus avoiding the hassle of renting and moving.

We moved Chris from Dallas to Indianapolis then to Denver, back to Texas and blessedly left his things in storage when he played in San Diego. I spent a lot of time on the road with Brittany, Chris's childhood sweetheart (they met in nursery school) who is now his wife.

Chris graduated from the University of Arizona in December 2009. Football season was over, and Chris and Rob left Arizona and went directly to Miami to train for the February NFL Combine, where promising players were invited to prepare for the upcoming NFL draft in April 2010. Brittany had just graduated from Arizona State in Phoenix and needed to bring her car and dogs back home to Buffalo, so I flew out to meet her in Tucson, and we drove Chris's and Rob's things in her car the thirty-four-hour trip to New York with two overnight stops. Their shoes alone, size 15 for Chris and size 17 for Rob, took up entire suitcases. We called this trip the Christmas Express. Brittany and I stayed at one hole-in-the-wall motel where we shared a room, one bed with three dogs and I slept with my hoodie up and my hands pulled into my sleeves and my socks and pants on. I didn't want to touch anything, but I was just so exhausted.

At one point as we traveled through New Mexico near the Mexican border, we reached a traffic stop, and I saw the cops going through people's cars. I realized that the giant cans of protein powder that we had consolidated into plastic bags for easy transport could be mistaken for drugs. I was so nervous that we would be arrested and thrown in jail. Luckily, the shift must have ended just as we reached them; the cops just got in their cars and left.

Further driving adventures with Brittany include the time we carted several buckets of exotic fish from Denver to Dallas. We started out with a twenty-six-foot truck that was supposed to be packed by professional movers. This load consisted of an entire household of furniture, clothing, sports gear, and the fish. Well, they didn't do a very good job, and all the stuff didn't fit in this truck, so we needed to rent an additional van, thus making it necessary for both of us to drive the entire trip.

We had packed the fish in the buckets last, and as we were driving our separate vehicles, we both discovered the fish were jumping out of the buckets. How do you get a fish off the floor of the car while driving? We had to pull over, rearrange everything, and get those buckets covered, yet somehow they were still escaping. These fish, by the way, were just one of Chris and Brittany's projects to earn some money while they were studying. This was their investment sloshing out of those buckets, so we had to be creative and save those fish. Luckily, we arrived in Dallas one day later than expected, exhausted (again) and only lost a few of the expensive little swimmers.

Gordie was a minimalist. Most of his belongings fit in the trunk of his car. We only did the big drive to Jacksonville once, then after that, he kept his things in storage as he went back and forth to Buffalo. Glenn was happy to have me help him settle into his current place in Dallas by bringing a truckload of furniture he "shopped" for at my house. And even though Rob has plenty of budget to hire people, he still stopped to pick me up at my house in Fort Myers on his way from Miami to Tampa, where he was having other furniture delivered to his new place. It took us about eighteen hours to get the place set up, including a run to the store for sheets and towels. Hey, I've got my scissors, my packing tape, some markers, and I'm ready to move whoever needs moving. It's all part of my job as Mama Gronk.

OUTNUMBERED

Lately, as my friends' daughters are getting married and having babies, I think about how different our lives, mine especially, would have been if we had another girl on the roster besides me. I am blessed to have two lovely daughters-in-law so far and even a baby grand-daughter, but it's not the same as having a daughter of your own. The what-if scenario is very real to me as my sixth pregnancy ended in miscarriage and I found out later that the baby was a girl. This was so many years ago, but it's one of those heartbreaks that just stays with you. I wonder if she would have been sports crazy like her brothers, if they would have been protective of her. I can tell you that I would surely have dressed her in pink.

In the early days of parenthood, it is easy to feel overwhelmed, exhausted, cranky, grateful, exhausted, resentful, wiped out, and completely inadequate. Once you get the hang of it, being a mom is lots of fun, a constant challenge—and still exhausting. With each successive child, confidence is gained, wisdom attained, and coping strategies developed. I learned early on, in my testosterone-filled household, that the best defense is a good offense.

Like many of my peers, I got married right after college gradua-tion. Gordy was so different from me: I was shy and quiet; he was loud and extroverted. He was fun, and this seemed to be the logical next step in our lives. And the next logical step after that was to have a baby. I always knew I wanted a big family—I come from a family of six, and my parents came from large families. Siblings and cousins were an import-ant part of who I was, so I was pleased to begin the trip to motherhood.

What I did not expect was the need to move to another state for Gordy's job so soon after having our first son, Gordie Jr. We ended up living in a small apartment complex right off a busy road. My husband took our car to work every day, leaving me home with a tiny infant; and though I was never alone, I was lonely. The road was too busy for me to push the baby in his buggy, so we circled the apartment complex parking lot. At one point, a neighbor opened her door and yelled out that children were not allowed in the apartment complex. Well, nice to meet you too and thanks for the welcome! I could only talk to my mother, in Buffalo, after 11:00 p.m. when the long-distance phone rates were cheapest—this was long before cell phones and the internet—and even then, we had to keep those conversations short.

Despite the loneliness at the beginning, the babies kept coming, and I was sucked into the vortex of full-time motherhood. This was the job I knew I was prepared for. I never thought about the exact number of babies I would have; I just took what God gave me, including the loss of that girl. I like to think she might have had a calming influence on the guys, and certainly it would have been nice to have someone on my side, to even out the playing field a bit.

It would be years before we added a female to team Gronkowski—a dog named Rosie. Our first dog was male, and I even joked that the carnival goldfish, who lived for eight years, was a boy. The house was filled with energy, testosterone, sports equipment, and noise. I was so busy that I didn't even notice the chaos; I just kept moving.

As parents, I don't think my ex-husband or I can take all the credit for the fact that all five of our sons became professional athletes. I feel they did most of that work by themselves. You know the phrase "You can lead a horse to water, but you can't make him drink." As you would expect, we provided the framework: Gordy encouraging them as they got older and doing physical training in our basement gym; me feeding them well, getting them where they needed to be on time, teaching them the organizational skills that made our house run smoothly, and being there every day when they left the house and every day when they came home. My secret to success was a series of large calendars. Everything was written down and easy for all to see. We always knew who was where, when and how they would get there. Planning is one of my favorite things to do. I know that Rob, Chris, and Glenn rely on a similar system to keep their adult lives in order, and sometimes they even give me credit for this.

Over the years, two of my little monsters have married and now have little monsters of their own. If someone had shown me a crystal ball when my kids were small, and I could see our relationships now, I think I would have been devastated. Being left out of plans and activities is painful to me.

Life in our house was like a continuous hurricane, everyone and everything in constant motion. The boys played all kinds of games together, roughhousing, yelling, laughing. At the same time, I was cooking, cleaning, and packing up for the next practice or game.

My boys have always motivated one another—the competition in our house was constant and physical. There was always something flying through the air, someone on the ground beneath a couple of brothers. Even I fell victim to the chaos that reigned in our living room when I was trying to rest on the sofa, nursing a killer headache. We all know that trucks don't usually fly, but in my house, those heavy metal toy trucks did. I got smacked on the nose by one such flying truck, and it surely helped me forget the headache that put me on the sofa in the first place.

From high school sports to college to the pros, I came to learn that football especially is really a year-round sport. Sure they have a few lighter months in the spring, but fitness and nutrition are 24-7, 365 days. We have not had a family holiday dinner in nearly twenty years.

Preseason training starts in July, preseason games start in August, and then the main events begin. Not only do we have Sunday afternoon games and Monday night football; now they have added Thursday night games to the schedule and even some Saturdays. It seems that fans of the NFL can't get enough football! That's a grueling 256 regular games per season with each team playing sixteen games in seventeen weeks. Now add preseason, playoffs, travel, practices, and team meetings to this number and you can see how a player doesn't have much time to see his family.

This is the main reason I didn't (and don't) go to many away games. The team arrives on the day before the game, checks into the hotel, goes to practice, has team meetings, eats dinner and then curfew. Sometimes there is an hour to visit with family and friends before curfew and lights-out. There are no late-night parties the night before a game. The hotel location is often a secret, and the players' floors are locked off and have security guards on duty. There are even bed checks for these grown men. When you think about it, these guys are an expensive investment for the team owners, and this must be a good way to protect that investment.

We don't get to see much of our players after an away game either. Rob will text me from the locker room, letting me know that he'll be out in ten minutes. It's everything I can do to push through the huge crowd waiting to see the players as they emerge from the locker room and get on the bus waiting to take them directly to the airport. I'm not particularly tall, but it usually works if I yell, "Hey, I'm Gronk's mom! Please let me through!" Most of the time, people will smile and let me through. Sometimes they even ask for my autograph. Can you imagine?

Home game seats are a little better than at away games. At home, the players get two free tickets, then they can buy tickets for family and friends, the cost coming right out of their paychecks. The cushy seats are reserved for corporate types and season ticket holders. There are no free tickets for away games.

Away games can be funny. The host team sets aside a block of seats for the visitors, for which payment is still taken from the players' paychecks. Usually, this block is very high in the stands, far away from the cheering hometown crowd.

Not everyone can turn on the TV to see what their kids are up to, and I have this interesting ability. Sometimes I don't want or need to know the many details that show up in front of me. The one thing that never gets old is that usually all five of those Gronkowski brothers are together. Whether it is the giant parade following a victorious Super Bowl for Rob or a sales pitch of Chris's Ice Shaker on the TV show *Shark Tank*, they are all together, mugging for the cameras, shoving one another, supporting one another, laughing and reveling in their brotherhood. Together and apart, they are all over social media, in the news, grabbing attention and enjoying the heck out of one another's company.

Along with the wrestling, teasing, and generally egging one another on, my boys supported one another too, and they still do. The younger ones have always looked up to big brother Gordie, and he has always been so good with them. He had an uncanny way of keeping everyone from killing one another and probably still enjoys his role as referee. Even as adults, those Gronkowski brothers reach out to one another for advice, help, camaraderie. It makes me feel so wonderful seeing them involved in one another's business ventures, showing up at football games, having a great time every time they get together.

5 Boys at Senior Bowl

"Who's your favorite?" they ask me in a teasing voice. Naturally, they don't expect an answer, and I don't give one. Rob always signs his cards to me, "From your favorite son." Glenn does the same and will give me a wink, like it's our secret. They certainly make me laugh, but I know they would probably be quick to talk me out of choosing a favorite. All for one and one for all.

I firmly believe that the success of all my sons is because they rely so much on one another. It didn't take long for them to stop coming to me for help with a problem; they took it to their brothers, their fraternity, their team. Slowly, I lost my position as captain. I know this is what every parent wants—a measure of success.

I almost always felt outnumbered, though they never ganged up on me. I had a green plastic spoon, often raised in warning, and the power to assign chores. They had a healthy respect for that green plastic spoon that I threatened them with. I used it only rarely, mostly because I couldn't catch any of them. And by the time I did catch one, they were usually laughing at something Rob did and we would all be distracted. I would beg them not to laugh at him, but they just couldn't stop; it was just encouraging him. He was (and is) such a goofball that even now he gets belly laughs from Glenn, just like when they were kids.

Even as grown-up men, my sons have had opportunities to gang up on me—all in good fun of course. As a team, they never tell on one another (and didn't when they were young), and they also never admit to any wrongdoing (and never did when they were young). Blame is easily dodged, even as they all tower over me and live in their own homes. When Mike and I got married, the boys stayed at our house in Florida and we went off to a nearby hotel after our wedding reception. When we came back to our house the next day, someone had thrown a banana against the wall and didn't clean it up. It turned black and was slowly running down the wall, and of course it stained the wall as it slid. At that time, I found out that you can't just wipe it off because when you do, the paint and some of the drywall comes with it.

Another fun wedding night surprise, compliments of my boys, was that they had "borrowed" a really nice golf trophy out of the venue where the wedding had been held and hid it in the trunk of our car. So, we had to take it back, kind of sneaky, and find one of the employees to help us get it back in before anybody knew it was missing. My boys do things like this and just laugh. I don't know who took the trophy or whose idea it was. I don't know who threw the banana on the wall, but if I asked, they would blame the brother who wasn't there. They have done this since they were small. That's stuff I don't need to know, and it really doesn't matter; these are things that I've just learned to deal with again and again with those guys. I don't know if a daughter would have done that… I kind of doubt it.

So back to my friends and their daughters. I envy their planning together and their closeness—it's just not the same for the mother of the groom. It's so nice that these daughters call their mothers looking for advice and help with wedding plans or questions about newborns. I always tell them to be sure to include their new son-in-law's mother in the planning. I know how important it is to feel part of the process and the excitement.

"It doesn't matter how good you are," I would tell my boys, "you are always part of a team and people rely on you." This applies to family, work, life in general. I've discovered how very true this is, as my position on team Gronkowski has certainly changed. I'm no longer the house mom for the fraternity, but I sure love to see them together.

The middle school years were when I learned to appreciate my "bleacher" friends. These are the people I would hang out with, fellow sports parents, changing from sport to sport, season to season. Bleacher friends are in some ways fair-weather friends: once it was off-season, I found they didn't call me anymore. Everyone was just so busy, but during the season, they were all the adult interaction you had. I loved my volunteer responsibilities at the concession stand, but I learned fast that all is not fair in love and sports parenting. Our house had a lovely in-ground pool and lots of room, so we would host many of the after-game parties. There, on showcase, were my five boys, in all their rambunctious glory. A particular memory stands out when Rob did a spectacular cannonball into the pool. The water shot out across the yard, soaking everyone, including those who were not wearing swimsuits. The soggy food in their hands, their dripping clothes and hair—nothing escaped that wave. The kids howled with laughter, while their parents smiled unconvincingly. *Come on*, I thought, *it's just water!*

The parties were fun, regardless, and I longed to be included in other events where I didn't have to do the setting up and cleaning up. There were plenty of mothers who would not return the favor, because, well, they had seen my five boys together and, quite simply, they could not handle the tribe that my family represented. It took me awhile to catch on, but when I did, it made me sad and a little angry.

My mother taught me to keep a neat and tidy home. I did this, without much thought for the time that I could spend on myself. Meanwhile, my neighbor had a messy house, but she took her kids to the museum and to the zoo and did crafts with them in her kitchen. As she was living her best life, I was nearly paralyzed with envy. But then again, she didn't have five sons. I certainly threw tennis balls in the backyard and wrestled with my crew, but I always had something else to plan and get ready.

WHY I WORE A HARD HAT
WHILE BREASTFEEDING

If it didn't require so much concentration, I would have laughed at myself trying to breastfeed an infant, diaper another, and find a sock for his brother, all at the same time. I needed excellent balance and coordination to do these things one-handed, leaning with the added weight of an attached, helpless human. Motherhood is glorious, but it is also really hard.

Breastfeeding is a wonderful and important part of taking care of your infant. It's also painful, time consuming, and tough to manage when you've got more than one child in the house. Let's talk about teeth. Of course when they're tiny, those perfect, adorable little babies have only gums with which to take nourishment. When you're nursing them, you're looking down at their cute little nose, marveling at their tiny hands. Then, somewhere around four months old, they bite you. So, it was sort of a Pavlov kind of thing to train them not to bite you while they're drinking.

It was necessary to manage our schedule around breastfeeding. I'm not just talking about getting the kids to school and doing the grocery shopping but even just managing to take a shower myself. When I finally did find a few minutes to do this, I had to time it very carefully. There I stood, under the blissfully hot water, looking at my stomach, which looked just like the road map of the United States with all the stretch marks. And then, of course, I'm full of milk, so when the warm water hits me, the milk just shot straight out of my breasts at a ninety-degree angle and covered the shower wall. So, I'm standing there thinking, *When did I become a cow?* It was rough when the grocery shopping took just a little too long, and I knew it was time for the baby to eat because I was full all the way up to my shoulders and it hurt.

Sometimes it was just nice to sit for a moment to feed one of those babies. He would be drinking, not biting, and I'd be watching the other kids running around while I was holding this little baby. And all of a sudden, a toy comes flying through the air, so I had to be the protector. Then when those nursing babies got a little older, it was easy for them to reach up and rip my earring out of my ear or pull my hair, all the while sucking and looking up at me so sweetly. That was when I cut my hair shorter and stopped wearing jewelry.

A benefit of nursing my babies actually wasn't that positive for me all the time as I became the permanent designated driver. So, if you're going out with a group of people, maybe one of the guys would drive to wherever we were going, but I always got to drive home. Usually, I didn't mind, but sometimes it was just too much. Like when it's two in the morning and everyone's calling out for "one more drink," and they're laughing at stuff that just isn't funny. And all I wanted to do was lie down on the floor in the restaurant or bar and just fall asleep. Often, I felt that if I was going to go out, pay a babysitter, I would have been better off just staying home, going to bed, and getting some sleep.

This is one of the joys of motherhood that I think my daughter-in-laws are figuring out now. You know that you're the one who gets up in the middle of the night and everyone thinks the baby slept through the night, and that's not usually true. I would be up at two, again at five and slept in the chair between those hours. Luckily, this stage doesn't last too long. Then you move onto other reasons for losing sleep, especially when they become teenagers and start driving cars.

DR. MOM

There is nothing worse than watching helplessly from the sidelines as your darling, grown-up child writhes in agony on the forty-yard line. Well, actually, what might be worse is discovering that one of your boys had been nursing a broken wrist for two weeks before you finally got a glimpse of the swollen mess that he had been hiding under a long-sleeved sweatshirt. (His philosophy, Chris assured me, was that it would just go away eventually.)

The ever-brawling, always-moving Gronkowski brothers spent surprisingly few hours in the emergency room as they were growing up, though we did spend one memorable Christmas Eve there. You would have expected me to be on a first-name basis with the hospital staff and local orthopedists, but very fortunately, that was not the case. My boys just didn't need to go to the doctor for sick visits. We were lucky with that. We didn't start seeing scary injuries until the guys were into college-level sports. Let's face it, being a kid is generally about always being a heartbeat away from some sort of injury. I've been able to rely on my calm center and the sense that there are only some things I can control in life.

While golf is not generally known for its injuries, Gordie managed to suffer a concussion while playing on the high school team. One of his buddies hit him in the temple with the handle end of the club. It was in a perfect spot to make him pass out. We went to the doctor, and he threw up all over the parking lot. They told me to wake him up every hour all night long. He slept with me as my husband was away. I set the alarm for every hour, but he ended up waking me because I was so exhausted that I didn't hear the alarm that was twelve inches from my head.

Then there was the time in Dan's senior year of high school when he hurt his knee and was in for an x-ray. The doctor came in to see us and explained that the injury required surgery and his football career was likely finished. So his father and I are trying to console him and point out that he's very smart, top of his class, and football would have to end at some point, so he should be positive about the future. We're all on the verge of tears when the doctor comes back in and apologizes. It seems he was looking at the wrong x-ray, actually that of a sixty-year-old man. Doc told Dan to go home, put some ice on the knee and he could go back to football the next week. Lesson here: check, double-check everything on medical records.

Next is Chris. In one of the very few times I didn't attend one of his hockey games, he traveled with another family to an away game. I wasn't at home taking a nap or out getting my nails done; I was at one of his brothers' events. About two weeks after this game, he tells me he has this bump on his arm. Turns out he got hit by a puck, between his wrist and his elbow pad and there was a bump where it shouldn't be. So, we go in for x-rays, and it was fractured. Even two weeks after the break, they put a cast on to protect it, so it wouldn't be reinjured. He had been playing basketball the whole two weeks before he got the cast. Within days, Chris had picked off the cast and was off doing whatever he wanted. I did manage, however, to get him to stop playing basketball for a while so the arm could heal.

Glenn, miraculously, escaped any major injury as he followed his brothers through a varied sports career. The only time he went to the hospital was on Christmas Eve when he was just a toddler. The older boys had been playing mini-hockey in the basement playroom, and Glenn just ended up in the wrong place at the wrong time. I arrived to blood everywhere as his chin was split open. Needless to say, we skipped Mass and Christmas Eve dinner that year. One sweet spot was when the hospital staff gave him a tiny stuffed teddy bear.

Over the years, I have watched my boys sustain a lot of injuries. I always try to be calm in the face of just about anything, and I've had a lot of practice doing that as they were growing up. All five take things as they come and don't overreact. I will admit, however, that my heart stops when there is a player laid flat on the field, not moving. When it is one of my own, I move into mom mode and quickly make my way to the sidelines. Rob used to be able to call me to let me know that he was okay when it was a minor injury, but now the process is much more complicated than it used to be.

My first experience with NFL injuries was when I was watching Dan on TV playing with the Broncos. I was at my house in Florida, not in the stands, so I didn't notice at first that there was a player down. I couldn't see his number out on the field and started to feel nervous about who might be on the ground, surrounded by coaches and trainers because I knew Dan had been in for that play. I'm relying on the cameraman at this point to show me if it's my son. They usually go to a commercial when a player is injured, then after the commercial, they show who got hurt. I waited forever. Yes, it was Dan, and luckily, he was able to walk off the field and sit on the bench for a while. Nowadays, I watch to see if they take a player directly to the locker room, in need of further investigation, or to the blue tent, designated for concussion observation.

Chris sustained a serious injury to his shoulder while playing for the Colts. He got hit with a helmet right in his shoulder, and it ripped his muscles apart. I joined his wife, Brittany, in Pensacola, Florida, for the surgery, which was really interesting because we actually got to watch the procedure as the doctor was working on him. It gets a little crazy when you see the doctor pull out a hammer and screwdriver and start hammering on your child's shoulder.

With more years in the pros, I was usually in direct contact with the Patriots' team security when Rob went down on the field. I'd go from my seat in the stands to the locker room where team doctors were examining him. The most memorable event was when he suffered a massive concussion and couldn't figure out why I was there, even though he had arranged the tickets and we traveled to the stadium together.

When Rob took that soul-crushing, helmet-to-helmet hit in the 2018 AFC championship game and just went down, I knew he was in trouble. They took him off the field and directly to the blue tent, which is specifically designated for serious injury review and concussion protocol. By the time I got there, he had been moved to the locker room and the doctors were talking about sending him right home, not back out onto the field. The decision to send him home took place before the game ended, so he could avoid the crowds. He asked me for my scarf, but I could not imagine why. When I gave it to him, he wrapped it around his head and face to disguise himself from the crowd and hustled out to the players' parking lot, hunched over to hide his height. He was under strict orders to go home and be very quiet for at least twenty-four hours, no TV, no phone, no loud conversations, no stimulation of any kind. Rob has always had great respect for the advice he gets around an injury. He does what he has to do to get back on the field as soon as he can.

Nothing compares, however, to the injuries Rob sustained in the 2013 matchup against the Cleveland Browns. He fell to a season-ending injury to his knee. There was so much attention paid to his ACL and MCL that nobody said much about the concussion he had at the same time. I know there is a lot of concern about concussions, and I have always felt my boys knew what they were getting into when they signed on to play this rough sport professionally. While I took comfort in knowing they always wore the best helmets, nothing prepared me for the scare I had when I finally got to Rob after that hit.

It took an agonizingly long time for the team medical staff to let me in to see Rob. He was stretched out on a gurney, and when he turned to look at me, his eyes were blank. For the first time, I was sick with fear. Those dark eyes, unseeing, not recognizing his mother, just scared the hell out of me. Eventually, he said in surprise, "Mom, when did you get here?" I was terrified by this as I had just been with him for a few hours before the game began.

Going to the hospital was surreal. I rode in the front of the ambulance and saw with disbelief that we were the only ones on the highway. All entrances had been blocked off by police, and two police motorcycles led the way straight to the emergency entrance. Guards were posted at the door, and Rob was assigned a number, which is how the medical staff referred to him the whole time he was there. All this to avoid the press. I couldn't believe how efficient this hospital visit was. If I needed a CAT scan, they would have told me to go home and I'd wait six weeks for an appointment. Rob's tests were done immediately, and with amazing speed, he was cleared to go home. The exit from the hospital was just like the entry—guards at the door. Rob was covered with a blanket and whisked through a back door, directly into the car.

WHEN DREAMS COME TRUE

(And Everyone Wants to Know if They Can Get Tickets)

What is it like to be the mom of one of the greatest NFL players currently on the field? To be the mom to not one but five sons who grew up to be professional athletes?

Sometimes it is overwhelming, often exhausting, and always interesting. I am so proud of all of them, and I'm so honored to have been part of their successes—and their failures too. As any good mom will lament, there is no guidebook or app to use for parenting. Most things are trial and error, experience, delight, and disappointment. Every day is different, and every day is a chance to improve on the day before.

People have been so excited about each of my kids' success. When each one entered the pros, we discovered a whole new, and previously unknown, group of friends and family. A cousin's boyfriend's housekeeper's son wanted to know, "Can I get tickets?" How about the classmate from kindergarten who didn't invite my kid to his birthday party who wants to know, "Can I get tickets?" Any tiny connection emboldens people to ask this question, and so many are shocked to hear, "No. Sorry." Even the lucky few who get a "yes" are astonished to learn that they are expected to pay for those tickets. Most people don't realize that the players don't get a slew of free tickets for every game. And the cost of those tickets comes right out of the players' paychecks.

As a mom, I do worry about people trying to take advantage of them. There are so many people out there that just want to get free tickets, free autographs, and free anything. I do realize that some of this comes with the job. But some individuals want to be friends just to advance their own careers. It does bother me to see them come out of nowhere to exploit the players for their own personal gain. And when the players are down and out, I wonder where those "friends" would be.

I must admit that, as I have logged more than twenty years as a football mom, I liked to sit in the Dunkin' Donuts corporate suite in the Patriots' Gillette Stadium rather than the nosebleed seats we endured at the very beginning, especially because we couldn't count on the weather. In Tampa, the club-level seats in the Buccaneers' Raymond James Stadium allow me to be with the fans and enjoy the energy of the game. I'm surrounded by folks sporting my son's number 87, and I love it.

Life as an NFL player's mom can be exciting, but some of the time, it is not. One minute, I'm standing next to my son, admiring his Super Bowl ring; and another, I'm fighting through a huge crowd after an away game just to steal a quick hug before he is on the team bus and whisked off to the airport.

Here is something that most people don't know about college and professional football: the players sleep in a hotel, secured by the team, before the games. They have curfews, bed checks, and even security guards posted near doors and elevators. This happens for every game—home and away, and also during preseason training camp. So, while I was staying at Rob's house, he was not there with me. But because he lived so close to the stadium, he could come home from practice to see me before heading to the hotel to sleep.

In the friends and family section at preseason practice, I sat on the grass, in the shade of a large white tent, and watched a couple of toddlers stretch out on the ground, roll down the hill, touch the fence, run back up the hill, and do it again, laughing hysterically the whole time. Behind me, their young moms talked, absently jiggling infants on their knees or caressing pregnant bellies. Looking at them made me think that those players out there on the practice field are very young guys. And no matter how good they are, this life as a professional football player can be very brief, and it is hard work. A fence separated the action zone of the practice field and the grassy hill where the toddlers rolled and the family members watched our players practice. Here I had the good fortune to see my two sons,

Rob and Glenn, run drills as members of the New England Patriots, preparing for a preseason game against the Jacksonville Jaguars the next day.

It never gets old for me to watch my boys play football. Even if I can't see the numbers on their jerseys, I can always tell who is who from a mile away by the way they walk. Glenn puts his hand to his mouth, Rob's walk has a very long pounding gait, Chris had a little shrug, Dan walked with composed dignity, and Gordie's long legs made him run like a giraffe.

When Rob and Glenn came off the field, we met at the fence, and both gave me a hug. Rob moved on, with Coach Bill Belichik and teammate Tom Brady to shake hands with visitors, VIPs, and other players' family members. Glenn stayed with me, watching Rob walk away. Glenn was on trial, not yet part of the team's regular roster; Rob, the experienced veteran. What a mom moment for me! We got together later at Rob's house, where Glenn was living during his tryout period with the Pats. It is amazing to me that three of my four NFL player sons have been on the Patriots roster, Dan for a short time in 2011. When Chris played for the Broncos, he played against his brother Rob and the Patriots in 2012.

Diane in Dunkin Donuts Suite in Gillette Stadium

I really enjoy preseason games, and I have been given a special treat for this one: Rob reserved seats for me, my friend, and Glenn's girlfriend, Regan, in the Dunkin' Donuts corporate suite at Gillette Stadium. He was a popular spokesman for them for a few years, and this turned out to be a "sweet" benefit for me. When I arrived at the suite, I found a half dozen Pop Warner (think Little League football) cheerleaders and their moms sitting in the seats reserved for my group. They were watching a huge crowd of slightly older cheerleaders, looking so tiny, down on the field delivering a wonderful, game-opening performance. When the field emptied out, the girls turned their attention to the huge jars of candy and snacks that were laid out for guests in the suite. Sadly, and inexplicably, there were no doughnuts. We took the girls' place in our seats and did an equally enthusiastic job of watching Rob and Glenn and their Patriots make short work of those Jaguars.

After home games in Foxboro, the Patriots players join their families in the cavernous hallway near the locker room for a gigantic buffet dinner. Here I see the toddlers again, now nodding off in their strollers. Older siblings race around clutching ice cream cones. As I enjoy the food and take in the scene, I'm reminded of just how "exciting" it is to have an outing with young children. Glenn joins us, but Rob does not. Even though there are rules in place forbidding "fan" behavior like asking for autographs, it still happens, making it impossible for Rob to enjoy this meal with his family.

Back at the house, the guys are tired after days of practice in the hot sun. They have had a drug test that morning and stand side by side, describing this common occurrence. Though neither has cause for concern, Rob points out that these tests are a reminder of the serious business they are in. One false move and they are out. Preseason is important—what they eat, how they work out, everything they do on and off the field matters. After a brief visit, they are off to make curfew at the hotel less than a mile away. Even during his year of retirement before joining the Buccaneers, Rob underwent routine drug testing as required by the NFL for one year following a player's retirement.

This day reminds me of the grueling practice sessions my sons endured when they played football in high school. Called "two-a-days," it was exactly that: a morning session, an afternoon session, with a short break between for lunch. It was so hot in August, and our house was close to the school so any number of guys would show up to eat, enjoy some air-conditioning, sprawl on the family room floor to watch *Let's Make a Deal* on TV, then go back to the field for more practice. Their dedication at such a young age was inspiring. This stands out as one of the very important times it was for me to be a stay-at-home mom. I liked joining in on their conversations, getting to know my boys' friends, and I really enjoyed having a front-row seat at what would become a lifelong passion and livelihood for my sons.

Fast-forward in my life as a football mom to another stand-out moment: the NFL draft. The whole process takes three days. Day one, the first rounders get picked; day two is second and third rounders; day three is the nail-biter, when fourth through seventh round picks are announced. Rob was invited to participate in the draft held in NYC in 2010. The NFL invites those players they think will get picked in the first round. The NFL put up our whole family in a swanky midtown hotel, and we went to Radio City Music Hall for the event, waiting in the green room for the show to begin. Rob was not picked in the first round, so we went back to the hotel, disappointed, and returned hopeful for the next day. A highlight of the trip was a visit to the Empire State Building with a private group of potential draftees. Here we were, walking around New York City, a bunch of huge, young guys and their families, all looking up, with our mouths open just a bit.

The next day, Rob was picked at the beginning of round 2. What a moment: at age twenty, he could not buy himself a beer, but he was at the start of an important career with one of the all-time great coaches on a winning team. And since he wasn't twenty-one years old yet, I had to sign his contract. Our family was jubilant, hugging, yelling, high-fiving. I was mostly smooshed between those big arms and wide chests. Here was my "little" boy, sporting his brand-new Patriots hat, experiencing one of the highest points in a pro football player's career. At this age, most NFL hopefuls had not even started playing in college.

While Rob's spot was secured, we still had one more Gronkowski waiting on draft news that year. Gordie, Chris, Glenn, and I left that evening to go back to Buffalo. We drove at night so we could be home in the morning to watch day three of the draft on TV. Chris was still waiting for his call. He did not get drafted but was picked up by Dallas at the end of the draft. He played a year for the Cowboys and started almost every game. This was the beginning of his 3.5 years in the pros. Then Glenn had his chance in 2016. The Buffalo Bills picked him up after the draft. So, Rob and Dan were drafted; Chris and Glenn were not but were picked up as free agents. Chris actually had a better NFL career than Dan. So, being drafted doesn't necessarily mean you will get time on the field or have a lengthy career.

Dan, Chris, and Glenn were not invited to the draft. For each of them, we watched on TV, and they had their phones in hand, waiting to get the call from the team that wanted to pick them up. In 2009, Dan got the call toward the conclusion of the draft, and we were overjoyed that the Detroit Lions were on the other end of the phone.

Of course, the top game of every year is the Super Bowl, and it is one amazing experience. I still can't believe that I can say "the first time Rob played in the Super Bowl" was number 46 against the New York Giants in Indianapolis. This would be the first of six trips to the Super Bowl—so far. I was so thrilled for him and a little overwhelmed by it all. The players do not get unlimited access to tickets, so I had to compete with his brothers, friends, rest of the family. I was so happy to go and witness the ultimate football-mom moment. Our seats were great, but it was so different from a regular game as we were surrounded by people who didn't care who won. They were mostly corporate guests and kept asking me who they should root for. The Super Bowl is only for the lucky few true fans of a team; for the rest of the people in the stadium, it is an exciting social event.

Ahead of time, one of the TV stations wanted to know where my seat was. When I got there, it was marked with a huge taped X, so they could zoom in on me. They do this for celebrities and other people who might be interesting when the networks cover the big games. Rob didn't play much because of an ankle injury, so I don't think I made it into the broadcast. That was the only time I had an X on my seat.

I really enjoyed attending the 2018 Super Bowl game, despite the disappointing outcome. Though it was February in freezing cold Minnesota, the dome was closed, so I didn't need eighteen layers of clothes and my earmuffs. It was a blast to attend the many family-oriented activities put on by the NFL for the fans and separately for each team's families. Super Bowl festivities each year include a welcome party with live bands, food, drinks, and a bus to the NFL Experience where the streets were blocked by security. One day after practice, each team got time to spend on the field for family photos. There was a breakfast on the day of the game, a hospitality room at the hotel, including activities for the little kids. The players didn't get to participate in any of this. They even had their own stairways and elevators in their hotel to get to where they needed to go for the important business at hand to shield them from being accosted by adoring fans.

A totally mind-blowing mom moment occurred in the NFL store at Gillette Stadium. I was surrounded by Patriots' gear and hundreds of shirts, sweatshirts, jackets, and hats bearing the number 87 and name Gronkowski. I saw little kids with Gronk hoodies and good-looking women in sexy tank tops with my son's face on them. There was even a bobblehead doll of my Rob. My goofball, always-brawling-with-his-brothers, all-pro, adorable son is a hero to thousands of strangers. Wow.

During the 2018–19 season, my husband, Mike, and I went to see Rob and the Patriots play the Buccaneers in Tampa, a rare but easy away game for us because we live just a few hours across the state. Who knew this would become a wonderful habit? This was a gorgeous fall evening, and I looked around at the packed stadium. More than half of the fans were there for the Patriots, and at least three quarters of those people were wearing #87 jerseys. I just could not get over it.

I've met some very interesting and famous people in my role as Gronk's mom. There was a time I joined a few other NFL moms for an ESPN special hosted by Annie Apple, mom of NY Giants Eli Apple. I sat next to Karen Flacco (Joe Flacco, Ravens), Dawn Elliott (Ezekiel Elliott, Cowboys), Cherie Shepard (Sterling Shepard, Giants), Penny Bennett (Martellus Bennett, Patriots; and Michael Bennett, Seahawks). Karen and I were the only moms of nonrookie players. We talked about the demands and joys of being mother to an NFL player. It was really nice to meet these ladies—my peers. It was very interesting for me to hear what their thoughts and experiences were, similar to mine and very different too.

I've been interviewed by Sports Illustrated, ESPN, the *Boston Herald*, the *Naples Daily News*, the *NBC Today Show*, and *Entertainment Tonight*. It took a lot of getting used to—I never knew exactly how to answer. Should I just give it to them exactly how I feel? I know that anything I said (or say) reflects on Rob especially, so I don't mind keeping a low profile most of the time. At one time, the Patriots website featured a video of a guy making my buffalo chicken wing dip. Can you imagine?

One particularly memorable Mothers' Day, I shared a stage with Alma Wahlberg, mother of actors Mark and Donnie, chef Paul, and Jimmy. Rob had invited me to join him for this event at the Foxwoods Casino in Connecticut as part of their Connecting the Stars Series, celebrity mothers' panel. The organizers flew me down from Buffalo and put me up in a beautiful hotel room.

Well, I was quite the rookie when it came to such an event, so of course I was a little nervous. I had my own dressing room and there were three gorgeous bouquets of flowers from my boys. I took all those flowers home with me.

Alma and I sat side by side on these huge white upholstered chairs in the middle of the stage. There were a couple hundred people in the audience, and we answered questions posed by a moderator. Luckily, we had received the questions in advance, so I had some idea of what I was going to say. The organizers asked us to send along ten photos that they would show on a screen behind us. Here was my rookie move: I sent ten. Alma sent about one hundred. When she came onstage, she got a rousing greeting from her hometown crowd. My microphone wasn't working, so answering those questions was a little tough, until Rob, Gordie, and Dan came onstage and the attention shifted to Rob. He played "Happy Mothers' Day to You" on the piano, to the tune of "Happy Birthday." Everyone got a real kick out of that. I even got paid for this appearance. Then we all went to dinner with Alma. It was just fantastic. After the show, my husband, Mike, and I went up to the high rollers' floor of the hotel to meet Rob, Gordie, and Dan. We arrived before the boys did and weren't exactly welcomed when we got there. The staff was hinting to us that this was the floor for high rollers and there was a minimum bet. I guess they judged me before they knew why I was there. Once I told them that I was meeting my sons, the Gronkowski brothers, suddenly it was okay. I think there is film of it on a *Walhburgers* episode. We took a lot of pictures, and it was just unforgettable.

After the Phoenix Super Bowl in 2015, the whole family went to Los Angeles and we made an appearance on the Jimmy Kimmel show. It is hard to describe how exciting and how fast these things go by. That same year, I went to the ESPN Espys Awards in Los Angeles where Rob was being honored as Best Comeback Athlete after sustaining so many injuries. There was a red carpet, and we got all dolled up. It was unreal to stand there for pictures, just like the Academy Awards.

And yes, I have met Coach Bill Belichik and team owner Robert Kraft a few times at Super Bowls. I met Tom Brady a few times as well. We spoke briefly, but there was always a crowd wanting his attention too. I would have liked

Diane @ ESPYS

to tell him that he has taught Rob so much but there is one thing that Rob has yet to learn: Tom Brady always says "Hi, Mom!" at the end of a TV interview. I watch for it. I would like to meet his mother one day. It's kind of like when the kids were small and I met all of their friends' moms when they would play together. Well, now I would like to meet the mom of Rob's friend!

I have a photo of myself with Rob and David Ortiz, also known as Big Papi, retired designated hitter for the Boston Red Sox. Rob and Big Papi were in Naples, Florida, shooting a commercial for Dunkin' Donuts a few years ago. I had a blast watching the whole process. It took all day to create a thirty-second commercial. One girl's job was to make sure the cup in Rob's hand was turned exactly the right way, the fake ice cubes perfectly placed, and the silicone "sweat" on the outside of the cup made that drink look truly ice-cold. There were tents set up all around the property of a huge house rented just for this commercial. Lunch was set out for the extras and the crew, and there were so many of them! Rob had to wear specific clothes in specific colors. It was just fascinating to see how much work goes into something that we only glance at. The icing on the cake was a mini photo shoot featuring Rob, Big Papi, and me.

Every year Rob shaves his head for the One Mission Buzz Off, to benefit childhood cancer research. This event happens across the country and is intended to show kids fighting cancer that they are not alone. One time, I had the honor of actually shaving Rob's head. I'm so proud of him and my boys for their work with their foundation Gronk Nation. Not a day goes by that I don't hear about another kind thing Rob has done to benefit a charity, cheer up a sick child, or teach young kids about the game he loves most.

I did enjoy going to Dallas, Detroit, and Indy also. They are indoor stadiums, which was great on hot or cold or rainy days. Also, the crowd was more likely to watch the game than to drink beer. It seemed that there was more "indoor" behavior at stadiums with a roof. I liked Denver when Dan, then Chris were playing there. And I'll never forget Rob playing in that Denver playoff game when a drunk guy dumped his beer down my back before we even sang the national anthem. And then he was yelling "Break Gronk's legs!" I was not excited to hear that and ended up watching the game on TV in the stadium hallway, which I suppose I could have done on my couch in Florida. Did I mention that I prefer home games?

Did you know that the families of Super Bowl teams often volunteer in the host city? In 2018 in Atlanta, Rob's last Super Bowl appearance with the New England Patriots, I loved joining in with the team's friends and family as we cooked, served, and socialized at the Atlanta Mission, one of the largest soup kitchens in the country. Moments like those are humbling and enlightening. What a wonderful way to engage with the city that welcomed thousands of football fans and enthusiasts for a weeklong celebration of the NFL's finest.

I suppose the greatest measure of my success as a mom is that my boys no longer need me, but they still need one another. It's gotten to the point where I'll turn on the TV or look online to see where my sons are and what they are doing. So often, I open the newspaper or see on Facebook, a photo of my boys together at a charity event. They live all over the country, but they get on planes to see one another. Right now, Rob is the focus as the last remaining NFL player, so the gang does their best to get to the games and cheer him on. I know he just loves that—to have his brothers by his side, each understanding exactly what it takes for him to do his job out there. They respect one another's work ethic, which I believe started when they were just little boys. And they still laugh at one another's jokes and pranks. Marriage, fatherhood, careers—nothing gets between those Gronkowski brothers.

Being a stay-at-home mom was very important to me and the most important job I have ever had. It is not glamorous, and there are no awards ceremonies for getting everyone to basketball practice on time. But it certainly is rewarding now to see my five boys succeeding where they want to succeed and still relying on one another for support and friendship. I think stay-at-home-mothers get a bad rap because so much of the job is behind the scenes and not easily measured. You don't get a raise if your kids get good grades. But you do get a raise, I suppose, when those good grades bring them a scholarship and better opportunities in the future.

Rob in Halloween Cow costume

There is no award for moms who bring up famous kids. But I will admit to feeling absolutely thrilled the first time I saw our name on an NFL stadium jumbotron. Rob is, by far, the most famous Gronkowski. He has always been popular with family and friends because of his fun-loving, always-positive attitude. I love that this has not changed as his fame increases, and so does his fortune. While his handsome face certainly sells a lot of Tide and helps his father's fitness business thrive, this fame also comes with a few less-than-positive side effects. Due to his size and recognizable mug, Rob can't go too far in public before someone spots him and asks for his autograph or a selfie. When he comes to visit me in Florida, we need to do a reconnaissance run before he can visit our community pool. If the group poolside has too many young twentysomethings, or too many men, all potential football fans, then Rob really can't go for a swim. Once he gets there, people are just all over him. So what do we do? We go to a friend's pool. Yes, this is the price of fame, but it is still a tough way to live sometimes.

When Chris got married in Dallas in 2015, he had begun his Everything Decorated.com business. His brother Rob was in his fifth season with the Patriots. It felt like the president of the United States was coming to the reception when you saw all of the security. There were absolutely no pictures or videos allowed (all guests left their phones at the door). This is because everyone shares everything on social media immediately, making it impossible to just relax and let loose, which my boys very much wanted to do. And did.

Going out to a restaurant often consists of a private room with a separate entrance or simply sending someone out for takeaway to eat at home. It is hard to hide when you are so much bigger than everyone else. In Boston especially, Rob was so well loved that people just came running when they saw him. He is usually very gracious, but sometimes, he just wants to be left alone.

I don't mind people recognizing my name and asking if I am *the* Mama Gronk. Actually, it is kind of fun. It just cracks me up that so many people are so surprised by how I look. I'm five foot six, medium build, brown hair, brown eyes, size 9 shoes. I think people expect me to be huge, but I'm not, and neither is their father. It must have been good prenatal vitamins, healthy food growing up, good physical fitness habits, and a fair bit of self-respect that produced these huge humans who accomplish such great things, on and off the playing field. I'm not above saying yes to the Dunkin' Donuts suite at Gillette Stadium or getting a discount on my car repair because the mechanic is a Buccaneers or Patriots fan. It's just fun. And like every other phase of life, the fame will fade, and I will still be Mama Gronk, known to the ones I love the most.

I discovered very early in Rob's career just how nasty football fans can be. When Rob and the Pats were playing in Buffalo, I wore my 87 jersey proudly and was cussed out by fans calling him (and me) a traitor, among other things, since he was originally from Buffalo, and I still lived there. Well, I wish I could have yelled back at them that it was actually the Bills who missed out by not drafting Rob. The Patriots won that game, and I learned a very important lesson about wearing the right shirt in the right town. The Bills did make a very good decision in 2016 by taking on Glenn; they just didn't keep him long enough.

My lesson here was that on the rare occasion that I did go to an away game for any of my boys, I wore a plain T-shirt.

WHEN I TRADE MY SNOW BOOTS FOR FLIP-FLOPS

Glenn playing for Buffalo Bills

The five-bedroom house on New Road we moved into in 2001 had an in-ground swimming pool, a tennis court that also doubled as a basketball court, a basement full of exercise equipment, two dogs, and approximately ten people sleeping there on any given night. My house was a cross between a sporting goods store, a youth hostel, a locker room, a cafeteria, and a gymnasium. It was often difficult to open the front door because of the many giant sneakers left in the way. I loved it.

By the time my youngest went off to college, that nest surely felt empty. All those chaotic, exhausting, exciting days had come to an abrupt stop. I could hear the clock ticking in the kitchen. The counters were spotless, the laundry finished. All household machines were quiet. I could even see to the back of the fridge. The second one in the garage was unplugged. There were flowers in the planters because I had time to tend them. Only one dog remained. Now there is time, now there is quiet, and it is bewildering and uncomfortable. It is as if the electricity was cut from a giant wind machine in a thumping disco, and it feels way too early to go home.

These small (then huge) humans were my life's work, all day every day for thirty-three years. There is no retirement party because you never leave the job of mom. In fact, the transition can be quite jarring. While their independence is certainly the ultimate parental goal, a mother's job is far from finished when those bedrooms are empty and the extra fridge is unplugged. She will continue to function for her family as life coach, cheerleader, and business consultant. Somewhere along the way, she might add "babysitter" and "grandmother" to her résumé while reclaiming her roles as travel agent, English teacher, chef, and art teacher.

Growing up in Buffalo, you don't really notice the relentless gray of winter, the piles of snow, the sloppy slush and heavy mud that is a sure sign of spring. It is simply part of the calendar, and you slog through. The sun would eventually come out for me; I just didn't know it yet.

Once the baby, Glenn, left for college, I got a job at a local grocery store (which I enjoyed very much) and spent free time with my sister and her husband, and that is how I met Mike, my husband.

We had known each other many years earlier when he was assistant coach for one of the boys' hockey teams. I thought he was a player's dad. He was very quiet and kept to himself. We met again at a rainy bus stop after a concert. (Sounds like a country music song, huh?) We got to chatting, went out for a couple of meals, and found that we really connected. He is completely different from my first go-round in the marriage department. Mike is quiet, reserved, and very thoughtful. He is caring and respectful of women, his mother and sisters, and especially me. He gives me credit for all I've done and the sacrifices I've made to raise my sons. He has no children from any previous relationship, and he gets along great with my boys—sometimes better than I do! We make a great team and enjoy working together at our thriving home watch business. He is an engineer, so he easily handles the repairs, wonky air conditioners, leaky sinks; I do the cleaning, managing, and arranging of services—for people who live in our Florida community dividing their time between the Sunshine State and other places, like Michigan and New York. Together we are problem solvers, and we have a lot of fun too. He is my husband and my biggest fan. I'm so happy to share the rest of my life with him. I had spent 100 percent of my middle years on those boys; now I can enjoy life with my best friend.

After my divorce from their father, I continued to travel to see the boys play in five different states.

In 2012 all five sons were in different states. Gordie, age twenty-nine, in Ohio, working for his dad; Dan, age twenty-seven, released from the Cleveland Browns, moved back to Buffalo; Chris, age twenty-six, was in Denver playing for the Broncos; Rob, age twenty-three, was in his third year as tight end for the Patriots; and Glenn, age nineteen, had begun his college football career at Kansas State University. Instead of driving vans full of teenagers to sporting events, I found myself driving alone to those fields or to the airport or to work. I stayed in hotels; I visited friends. I was not yet remarried, so it was often a lonely point of transition in my life. I continued to do what I did naturally: kept moving and did my best to see every one of my boys on whatever field they were scheduled to play.

At this time, I was managing to travel to all those places to see three NFL sons and one college guy tear up the grid iron. When I went to Indianapolis to visit Chris, I loved the beautiful new indoor stadium, where the Super Bowl was played that year. I was always excited to go to a place for the first time: what would I find there that I was not expecting? In Denver, the stadium is gorgeous, but the neighborhood is not impressive. I had no problem breathing in

Colorado, despite warnings to the contrary. In San Diego, I loved the bay and the ships. The Dallas stadium is enormous, and the jumbotron was distracting and so distinctly detailed.

Even though I am the mom of four NFL players, and one MLB player, there is usually no fifty-yard line luxury box where you sit on cushy seats and someone brings you gourmet food. There is no helicopter arrival and golf cart delivery to the stadium. I parked my car a mile away, paid a fortune for the privilege, and hiked my way to get in line to have my clear plastic handbag checked only to have my long-forgotten airline peanuts taken away from me. You can't bring food into the stadium.

After sixteen years as a professional sports mom with dozens of jerseys with my last name on them, my last remaining NFL star buys the tickets for me in the protected part of the arena so I can watch him lead the Bucs to victory in a more comfortable environment. I still have to travel, deal with security and check-in lines, but at least the seats are warm and I don't have snow on my shoulders.

Tailgating did not become its own sport for me until the guys turned pro. When the guys played football in high school, I coordinated the huge, season-opening family picnic; and for college games, we just did snacks and took our player and his friends out for dinner whenever we could. The more pro games I attended as an NFL mom, the more pro I became at putting together a tailgate party.

When my husband, Mike, and I go to an away game and we are traveling by plane, I pack a cooler bag in my checked luggage. It usually contains important family favorites: frozen Sahlen's hot dogs, homemade chicken dip, and a few jars of my strawberry jam. It's funny, not once has the TSA actually questioned me, but I'm sure they wonder what the heck I'm doing with this stuff in my suitcase. Once I get to my destination, I hit the local grocery store for anything else that we need to fulfill our tailgating needs. I always get a veggie platter because I feel guilty about eating all the rest of that unhealthy stuff.

Diane & Mike (as News anchors)

In Boston, we would get one parking spot right next to Gillette stadium to stage our tailgate. Others parked across the street at a car dealership and hiked to the stadium parking lot. Usually, we had a large crowd of family, and friends huddled under our tent. The grill was going, folks were wearing their #87 gear, and we had a great time.

For the 2020 season, the COVID-19 pandemic certainly made things difficult as we began our career as a Bucs family. Despite the limits on fan attendance, we were lucky to attend every Bucs home game. We wore masks and filled out the health questionnaire. We sat in pods of two or four, with empty rows all around us. It was actually kind of nice, especially because there was no one sitting near me with an open beer.

Nowadays, whenever I'm on the road, I always have a peanut butter and jelly sandwich in my backpack. After so many years of doing this, I guess old habits die hard. I'll say, we have been saved by this on more than one occasion when we were stuck in traffic, stuck on a plane, or in the middle of nowhere with no restaurants in sight. You just never know. Mike and I recently pulled over on the side of the road and enjoyed our PB&J while running from one hockey rink to another. He still coaches hockey after thirty-plus years.

Diane & Rob after Tampa Bay Super Bowl 2020

With all the success I have witnessed via my professional athlete sons, you might wonder, what could be on my bucket list? I would like to be in a Campbell's soup commercial, I'd to like fly first class on an airplane, and I'd like to visit all thirty-one NFL stadiums.

Although there are thirty-two teams, the NY Jets and the NY Giants share a stadium, which is not in NY at all but in NJ. I have gone to Dallas, Denver, Washington, Cleveland, Detroit, Kansas City, Atlanta, New England, Miami, Pittsburgh, Indianapolis, Baltimore, New Orleans, Giants/Jets, Buffalo, Tampa, Jacksonville, Arizona, Minnesota, Houston, and the Chargers when they were in San Diego and Chris played there. They are now the LA Chargers, so that would be twenty-one. I am missing ten, which includes Carolina, Seattle, Green Bay, San Francisco, Philadelphia, LA Rams, Tennessee, Oakland, Cincinnati, and Chicago (2019 season).

Since that hurricane of child-rearing has blown through my life and all is calm, I pick through the rubble, looking for the things I would like to do next.

All 5 boys wore this outfit home from the hospital when they were born. Now my grandchildren are wearing it home.

This book is my call to action. I've been thinking about it for a long time. So many people who meet me ask, "How did you do it?" And the next thing they say is, "You should write a book." Well, I've heard that enough times to realize that maybe this is a good idea. From my vantage point, I can tell you that I strongly feel that stay-at-home parents do not get enough credit. My goal is to see that they do get the recognition and support they deserve and the encouragement to take on this job. 24-7 parenting is not for the faint of heart, but it is one of the most important things a person can do—for their children, for their family, and for the future of our country. If we can raise confident, intelligent, respectful young people, imagine what the world will look like.

End

Arcade

Mike and Diane

Chris and Rob

Rob as bare butt rider.

Boys with Dustin

Recipe Section

BUSTER BARS

8 oz. Oreo cookies
1/4 cup melted margarine
1/2 gallon Vanilla Ice Cream
2 cups confectioners sugar
1 can evaporated milk
2/3 cup chocolate chips
1/2 cup margarine
8 oz. cool whip
salted peanuts (optional)

Crush 8-oz. Oreo cookies
Mix well with 1/4 cup margarine, melted. Press into a 9x13 pan.
Spread 1/2 gal. softened vanilla ice cream on top, freeze.

Mix together and cook for 8 minutes (until it thickens kind of like a pudding):
2 cups confectioners sugar, 1 can of evaporated milk
2/3 cups chocolate chips, 1/2 cups margarine.
Cool, then spread over top of ice cream. Return to freezer. Top with 8 ounces of cool whip.
Sprinkle with salted peanuts.
(You can use different kinds of ice cream like butter almond or butter pecan in place of vanilla,
or you could try cookies and cream ice cream in place of Oreos and vanilla ice cream.)

Who doesn't love this?
Chocolate!

TEXAS SHEET CAKE

Boil:

    2 sticks margarine (or 1 cup cooking oil)

    1 cup water

    4 tbsp. cocoa

Add:

    2 cups flour

    2 cups sugar

    1/2 tsp. salt

Mix together then add:

    2 beaten eggs mixed with 1/2 cup sour cream (or buttermilk) and 1 tsp. baking soda

    Beat well. Pour into greased and floured 11x17 baking sheet.

Bake 375 degrees, 15–20 minutes.

While cake is baking:

    Heat 1 stick margarine, 4 tbsp. cocoa, 4–6 tbsp. milk to a boil. Remove from heat. Add 4 cups confectioner's sugar, 1 tsp. vanilla, 1 cup chopped nuts.

    Spread frosting on cake while it is still warm

    Goes a long way, I still make this for my neighbors. They have no idea how to make it.

CINNAMON COFFEE CAKE

1/2 cup shortening
3/4 cup sugar
1 tsp. vanilla
3 eggs
2 cups flour
1 tsp. baking powder
1 tsp. baking soda
3/4 tsp. salt
1 cup sour cream
6 tbsp. butter
1 cup brown sugar
2 tsp. cinnamon
1 cup chopped nuts

Cream the first three ingredients well. Add eggs one at a time, and beat well after each addition. Add dry ingredients and sour cream to creamed mixture, blending well. Grease bundt pan well with Crisco. Put half the creamed mixture in the pan then all the nut mixture (butter, brown sugar, cinnamon, and nuts) and then the remaining half of the creamed mixture.

Bake 350 degrees for 45–50 minutes.

Invert Bundt pan on to plater after sitting for 5 minutes.

Best ever! Family favorite between us sisters.

BLUEBERRY BUCKLE

Mix well: 3/4 cup sugar, 1/4 cup soft margarine, 1 egg

Stir in: 1/2 cup milk

Stir in: 2 cups flour, 2 tsp. baking powder, 1/2 tsp. salt

Carefully blend in 2 cups well-drained blueberries.

Pour into a 9-inch square pan.

Sprinkle top with crumb mixture: 1/2 cup sugar, 1/3 cup flour, 1/2 tsp cinnamon, and 1/4 cup soft butter.

Bake: 375 degrees, 45–50 minutes

I still make this and mail it to Chris. He always says that he "ate the whole thing in two days!"

FRESH APPLE CAKE

Serves 12

Pan coating:
3 tbsp. sugar
1 tsp. ground cinnamon

Cake:
1 1/2 cups vegetable oil
2 cups sugar
3 large eggs
3 cups chopped apples, peeled (about 3 medium apples)
3 tsp. vanilla extract
2 tsp. ground cinnamon
3 cups all-purpose flour
1 tsp. baking soda
1/2 tsp. salt
1 cup chopped walnuts

1. Preheat oven to 325 degrees
2. Generously grease a Bundt pan. Combine the sugar and cinnamon and coat the inside of the pan with the mixture by shaking the pan all around until the sides and bottom are coated.
3. Beat the oil and sugar with an electric mixer until well blended. Add the eggs, one at a time, beating well after each addition.
4. With a spatula, stir in the apples and vanilla.
5. Sift together the cinnamon, flour, baking soda, and salt. Add the flour mixture to the apple mixture and mix well with a spatula.
6. Add the walnuts. The batter will be very thick.
7. Spoon the batter into the prepared pan and smooth the top.

8. Lift the pan from the counter about 2 inches and drop it back down to get out all of the air bubbles.
9. Bake the cake for 1 1/2 to 1 3/4 hour until a toothpick inserted in the center comes out clean.
10. Allow to rest on the countertop for at least 30 minutes before turning out onto a cake plate to cool completely.

One of Dan's favorite!

HOLIDAY EGGNOG

6 eggs
1 cup sugar
1 1/2 qts. milk
3 cups heavy cream (whipped)

Beat egg yolks until thick and light. Add sugar gradually and chill for 1 hour. Then add milk slowly and fold in whipped cream and egg whites that were beaten stiff.

Chris was always in charge of the eggnog.

SINGLE PIE CRUST

1 1/3 cups flour
1 tsp. salt
1/3 cup oil
3 tbsp. cold milk

Mix together. Roll out dough, and then put in a pie pan. Bake at 400 degrees for 8–10 minutes.

FRESH APPLE PIE

6 cups of thinly sliced apples
1 cup sugar
2 tbsp. flour
1 tsp. cinnamon
1/8 tsp. salt
2 tbsp. oil
1 double-crust pie pastry

Heat oven to 425 degrees.

Peel and slice apples. Combine dry ingredients, and mix with apples to coat. Put into a pastry-lined 9-inch pie pan. Drizzle with oil. Cover with top crust; cut slits for steam to escape. Make a high-fluted rim. Bake for 35 to 45 minutes until nicely browned.

FRESH PEACH PIE

4 cups of peaches
3/4 to 1 cup sugar
4 tbsp. flour
1/2 tsp. cinnamon
1 tbsp. oil
1 double-crust pie pastry

Heat oven to 425 degrees.

Peel and slice peaches. Combine dry ingredients; mix with peaches to coat. Put into a pastry-lined 9-inch pie pan. Drizzle with oil. Cover with top crust; cut slits for steam to escape. Bake for 35 to 45 minutes.

ZUCCHINI BREAD

2 cups grated zucchini
3 1/2 cups flour
4 eggs
1 1/2 tsp. baking soda
2 cups sugar
1 tsp. salt
1 cup oil
1 1/2 tsp. cinnamon
1 tsp. vanilla (mix together)
3/4 tsp. powder
1 cup walnuts

Mix ingredients together, pour into 2 greased loaf pans and bake in preheated 350-degree oven for 55 minutes (cupcakes approx. 25 minutes).

Gordie's college roommates were crazy about this and wanted me to bring it every time I came to visit.

PEANUT BLOSSOMS

1 3/4 cups flour
1 tsp. soda
1/2 tsp. salt
1/2 cup sugar
1/2 cup packed brown sugar
1/2 cup shortening
1/2 cup peanut butter
1 egg
2 tbsp. milk
1 tsp. vanilla
48 milk chocolate candy kisses

Combine all ingredients in a large mixer bowl (except for candy kisses). Mix on the lowest speed until dough forms. Shape dough into balls using a round teaspoonful for each. Roll balls in sugar and place on ungreased cookie sheets.

Bake at 350 degrees for 10–12 minutes. Top each cookie immediately with a candy kiss, press down firmly so the cookie cracks around the edge.

Everyone's favorites—Unwrap the kisses while on phone or watching TV (or riding in a car).

CHICKEN PIE

4 cups pepperidge farm dressing
2 sticks margarine
1 1/2–2 cups milk
4 cups diced cooked chicken
1 can cream celery soup
1 can cream of chicken soup
2 packages frozen peas and carrots (cooked)
1/2 cup chicken bouillon or stock
2 tsp. parsley

Melt margarine and mix well with dressing. Spread on bottom of the 9-by-13 pan, reserve 3/4 cup or more of dressing. Mix other ingredients, and pour over the dressing. Top with reserved dressing and sprinkle parsley flakes on top (may be refrigerated all night before baking). Bake at 350 degrees for 40 minutes. Bake longer if cold (about 1 hour).

CRANBERRY CHICKEN

1 can whole cranberry sauce
1 package dry onion soup mix
8-oz. Catalina dressing
4–5 chicken breats, cut in half

Mix first three ingredients together.
Add boneless chicken. Marinate (2 hours) and bake uncovered at 350 degrees for 1 hour.
Serve over rice.

Glenn makes this all the time—no cutting up or precooking!

BANANA BREAD

3 large bananas (very ripe)
2 eggs
2 cups flour
1 cup sugar
1 tsp. salt
1 tsp. baking soda
1/2 cups walnuts

Mix together. Bake 350 degrees in greased pan for 45–50 minutes.

I make a few hundred loaves every Fall. We give one to each of our customers when they return to Florida for the winter.

OVERNIGHT TOSSED SALAD

Begin this salad with the bottom layers of lettuce and build up each layer as follows:

1 head lettuce, cut up
3 stalks celery, chopped
3/4 of a large green pepper, chopped
1 medium red onion (or a regular one)
1 package frozen peas, cooked, drained, and cooled
1-pint miracle whip or mayonnaise
Parmesan cheese, sprinkled
1 1/2–2cups grated cheddar cheese
Cover and refrigerate overnight.

Toss before serving.

Everyone loves this! No need to have all flavors of salad dressings.

POTATO SUPREME

Use thawed frozen shredded potatoes (one large bag).

Mix with 2 cups shredded cheddar cheese
1-pint (2 cups) sour cream
1/3 cup chopped onion
1 stick melted margarine

Bake at 350 degrees for 45 minutes or longer
(can be frozen and reheated)

BAKED BONELESS CHICKEN BREASTS

(Dustin's Chicken)

3 boneless chicken breast
(cut in half)
6 slices Swiss cheese
1 can cream of chicken soup
2 cups Pepperidge Farm stuffing crumbs mixed with 1/4 lb. melted margarine

In a greased baking pan, arrange 6 pieces of chicken breasts. Place slices of cheese on top of each. Pour soup over the top—then buttered crumbs. Bake at 350 degrees.
1 <u>hour covered</u> with foil
<u>1/2 hour uncovered</u>

We call this "Dustin's Chicken." Gordie's friend, Dustin, lived with us for many years. This was his favorite, but the boys love it too.

MAMA GRONK'S FAMOUS CHICKEN SOUFFLÉ

(serves 8 or 4 *really* hungry teenagers)

8 slices of white or wheat
   bread, cubed
4 cups cooked, diced chicken
1 cup chopped celery
1 large white onion, chopped
1/2 cup mayo or Miracle
   Whip (I use Miracle
   Whip Light)
3 cups milk
4 eggs
1 can condensed cream of
   mushroom soup (I use
   Campbells)
3 cups grated cheddar cheese
   (use more or less to taste)

Chicken Soufflé recipe

Grease bottom of 9×13 pan. Line with 4 slices of cubed bread. Combine chicken, celery, onion, and mayo and spread over bread. Cover chicken mixture with the next 4 slices of cubed bread. Combine egg with milk and pour over top. Cover and let sit in refrigerator for several hours or overnight. Remove cover and bake for approximately 1 hour at 350°F, checking that the center is firm. Remove from oven, spread can of cream of mushroom soup on top, and then sprinkle the cheddar cheese on top of soup. Bake another 5–10 minutes, to melt cheese. Casserole will have puffed up, like a soufflé.

Tips: You could buy the onion and celery already chopped from the produce department or buy frozen onion. If you have leftover chicken from another meal, especially rotisserie chicken, cut it up and put it in the freezer for when you want to make the chicken soufflé recipe. Cooked soufflé can be frozen but may "deflate."

ABOUT THE AUTHOR

Diane Gronkowski was a stay-at-home mother of five sons, all of whom became professional athletes, with the odds of that being much greater than winning the lottery.

She dedicated many years of working 24/7/365 to keeping her "boys" organized, fed, educated, and on schedule.

Now, she lives in SW Florida and is remarried to Mike Walters.

Together they have a home watch business. She currently has eight grandchildren, with a prediction of many more to come.

Susan Irving Monshaw, a journalist and writer for more than thirty-five years, is an award-winning flash-fiction author who also loves to write about people. She pens a monthly blog, *Hither and Yon*, stemming from a decade-long stint as a weekly columnist for the *Citizen News* (New Fairfield, Connecticut). Having lived in New York, Paris, Tokyo, Chicago, and London, Susan loves to travel and writes often about those adventures for an international magazine.

CPSIA information can be obtained
at www.ICGtesting.com
Printed in the USA
LVHW071914180223
739850LV00021B/1368